What Kind of Woman Is This?

Unique Insights Into Proverbs 31
By a Modern 'Proverbs 31 Woman'

By

Shoddy Chase

What Kind of Woman Is This?
Unique Insights Into Proverbs 31
By a Modern 'Proverbs 31 Woman'
ISBN: 0-962-8168-0-9
Copyright © 1999 by Shoddy Chase
Keys to Freedom Ministries
P. O. Box 91995
Lakeland, FL 33804-1995

Text Design: Lisa Simpson

Printed in the United States of America.

Dedication

I dedicate this book to the two most beautiful women I know: my mother and my daughter Brittany. The love I feel for you both surpasses any love I could ever describe. So many love songs have been sung; yet the one I would sing for you has yet to be composed.

Contents

Contents

Acknowledgments

I would like to thank my husband Paul for always being there for me. What a faithful, honorable, hard-working man you are! You and I will forever be a team, but you're the best part of this team!

I would also like to thank my editor, Cynthia Hansen, for her diligence and for putting up with my humor.

Finally, to all the staff of New Life Christian Center, you're the best! Thank you for all the love, understanding, and commitment throughout the years.

Living the life
we were destined to live —
that's what this book
is all about. Through the
Word of God, we discover
that being a woman
is more than exciting —
it's amazing!

Introduction

I love to browse through a Bible bookstore. The copious collection of writings seems to almost hypnotize me. What is supposed to be a twenty-minute quick stop to buy a friend a gift often turns into hours of leisurely looking. Never mind that I left the car running or that three children have to be picked up from school. There's bookstore browsing to be done!

I enjoy looking through all those "positive potential" books, as well as books of poetry and books on prayer. Then there's always a host of "how-to" books filling the shelves, just begging to be explored. (I guess we need to learn *how to* before we can *do*. But so often we *don't* do what we *should* do or *could* do!) I also check out the systematic instructional manuals that we all need but rarely buy.

And did you know that in every Christian bookstore, there is an "Area 51"? (You know, that's the place where the U. S. government is rumored to hide aliens!) I'm talking about the "hush, hush" part of the store, a strange yet compelling aisle filled with silent bestsellers. More often then I would like to admit, I find myself among these menacing manuscripts.

Books you would love to buy but never admit to buying are down this aisle. Books with "Anonymous" written under their titles fill shelf after shelf.

Since you are a reader and known to be inquisitive, I thought you would be interested to know some of those books that have changed me forever and that, in all actuality, have made me who I am today (fortunately or unfortunately, however you may look at it!). They have enhanced my ministry and broadened my way of thinking. (Oh, boy! Now I *know* you'd like to get your hands on the "Area 51" bestseller list!)

I start with one of my favorites. It's an easy-reading book of about fifty pages, and the author's outlook is quite unusual. It's entitled *How To Understand Everything About Life: Dealing With Menstruation, Men, Marriage, Money, and Menopause* (in that order). Written by the famous preacher, Dr. Noitall, the book has a sequel that also really blessed me called *The Wrinkled Warrior: How To Grow Old and Still Be on Fire for God.*

The mentally stimulating, spiritually invigorating book *How Not To Be a Stupid Christian, Illiterate of the Bible, Embarrassing the Entire Kingdom of God* set me totally free. Another book, entitled *How To Deal With Your Seemingly Possessed Teenager,* was a big blessing to me as well.

The next book on my list, entitled *How To Tape Over and Sabotage Your Teenager's Evil Music While Letting Them Think It Is an Eerie Act of God,* was fabulous. I continue to use what I learned on a regular basis.

How Not To Slap Thy Neighbor saved my testimony before the community. And two books that I pass out like gospel tracts are entitled *How To Handle Depression After Hearing the Six O'clock Local News* and *How To Resist the Temptation To Call Dr. Kavorkian After Hearing the World News.* Then there's the book *How To Watch the Sicky Lake Show Without Cursing Her and All of Humanity,* which has nearly become a worshipped written work of art.

And, of course, no bookstore would be complete without testimonials such as *How I Lived With My Jerk Husband for Twenty-Five Years and Still Remained Saved* and *How I Coached Little League and Did Not Strangle Even One Obnoxious Parent.*

I want to mention one more book, which, by the way, was a textbook at our Bible school. As a minister myself, I must say this particular book has been my lifesaver. It's called *How To Live, Love, and Minister in a World of Stupid, Irresponsible, Hardheaded Imbeciles.* The author of that book remains anonymous. (I wonder why?)

If you are interested in books such as the ones I just mentioned, let me know. There are more books down that aisle than I care to mention, and more customers than I care to count!

If you can't find exactly what you're looking for on that "shady aisle," don't be discouraged. In most fine Christian bookstores, there are the well-lighted sections as well, where freedom from being jabbed in the eye from someone's elbow as they grab the newest release allures the sane and sober. You can meander for hours, prayerfully looking for that special book with hopes that its contents

contain some capsule of truth that will somehow shake up the reader.

So a trip to the bookstore is a great adventure to me. In fact, it often takes on the air of an exciting treasure hunt, because I know that the knowledge in some of those books on the shelf, if read and applied, can actually revolutionize a person's life.

The Purpose of This Book

The purpose of this book is to accomplish just that: the revolutionizing of your life! Does that sounds a bit grandiose? Well, then, on a more realistic level, I'd like to sensitize and energize your faith and love for Jesus. If I can accomplish that goal to even a small degree, I'll be happy.

In the actual writing of this book, I learned a great deal. For one thing, I discovered in a fresh, new way how timeless, tested, and true the Word of God is. God's Word is truly for all generations. If believed and acted upon, the Word will soften hardened hearts and produce miracles in people's lives.

A Christian author's dream is that this power in God's Word will touch the heart of whomever reads his or her book. It is the author's hope that by the time the reader finishes the book, he will be one step closer to the abundant life he desires — that realm where truth and joy abound and the meaning to life is understood more clearly.

It is also this author's dream that the reading of *What Kind of Woman Is This?* will help the weak to be made stronger; the undisciplined to find determination; the sad to find a laugh; those who struggle from a lack of purpose

to find their niche; and those who are far from God to be drawn nearer to Him.

More than anything else, dear reader, my desire for you is that you would feel the Presence of the Lord and be uplifted in heart as you read this book. I pray that the simple truths shared within these pages would make a mark in your spirit forever and open your eyes just a little wider to the wonderful Word of God, to our matchless Savior Jesus Christ, and to the supernatural work the Holy Spirit wants to do in you as you journey through life.

Help for the Journey Through Life

Reading can be a very effective tool to help us as we travel on that inevitable journey. It's a journey in which we will encounter a variety of terrains — smooth plains, rough and jagged roads, or dark and foreboding forests.

And at those times when the road abruptly turns and we find ourselves stuck in the mud, we will have the opportunity to learn a great deal about our own dispositions. Faced with unexpected inconvenience and unfamiliar surroundings, we may watch a hitherto-unknown and not-altogether-desirable facet of our personality emerge!

That's where the fun begins — a new leg of the journey in which much learning takes place. That's also where the tears may fall. How well we travel the bumpy spots in life reflects the condition of our spiritual "shock absorbers," also known as the love walk, the fruits of the Spirit, and Christian character.

The bumpy spots come to everyone on this journey through life. So I pray that my book makes the journey a

little easier for you as it strengthens your "inner vehicle" through a little humor, a lot of insightful reflection, and some good, old-fashioned godly wisdom.

Any wisdom I have to share with you has been acquired by walking closely with God for many years. He has traveled with me and brought me through a lot of unfamiliar territory of my own for more than two decades. I've also gleaned a measure of wisdom through the struggles of raising three wonderful children and through a life of serving God as I've waited for His promises to be revealed — just as you do.

But most of all, my desire is to share with you from wisdom placed by God's grace within a heart that cries out to be more like Jesus — a heart that realizes more than anything else my own human weaknesses and God's wonderful, endless mercy and love.

Laughter: The Key When Life Seems Too Serious

Friend, if any of the humor in my presentation of this message offends you, please forgive me. I would never use laughter to purposely belittle God's Word. I love to laugh and make others laugh as well, and I will forever find a way to be happy in the midst of all the heaviness in this world. As you know, life can be far too serious.

Proverbs 17:22 (KJV) says, *"A merry heart doeth good like a medicine: but a broken spirit* [a cranky and too-serious spirit] *drieth the bones."* It's a good thing the Bible encourages us to have a merry heart, because some of my favorite

people are a cross between Katherine Kuhlman and Erma Bombeck!

Have you ever been around people who "drieth up the bones"? You know the type I'm talking about. I call them "Mr. and Mrs. Bubble-Buster" — those who see the dark clouds coming ten thousand miles away and notice every imperfection in every situation.

God help you if sourballs like that live nearby — or, even worse, if *you* are just such a sourball! If that's the case, read this book quickly. It may not be too late to help you!

Why This Book?

I know there have been plenty of books written on the subject of Proverbs 31. I wrestled with that very fact as I prayed about the "why" of this endeavor. What would make my book different or special from all the others? Did I have anything to say that has not been said before? *Most likely not*, was the answer I received.

How silly my dilemma was! Are there not countless love songs that express similar thoughts and emotions, countless pieces of music that express a similar theme, and volumes upon volumes of books that are written on many similar subjects?

So what makes my book about the Proverbs 31 woman special? Only one thing: It is written by me.

You see, one day while praying about the writing of this book, I received a simple revelation: The Heavenly Father made each of His children a unique, one-of-a-kind creation, awesomely and incredibly designed for His divine purposes.

That revelation helped me understand how special and individual each of us is — including me! From that moment on, I knew that I had something to say about the Proverbs 31 woman and that it would be said in a way that only I could say it.

Not 'For Women Only'

By the way, this book of mine is *not* a "for-women-only" book. Men should also read it, because they, too, can benefit from its message.

You see, Proverbs 31 is part of God's Word. That means God intended it to be read by *all* of His children because there are no "gender-exclusive" books in the Bible. So if you are a male reader, do me a favor and read this "book for everybody." Then let me know what you think of it!

As for my female reader — you and I have so much in common, and it's from a woman's heart that I write to you. Truthfully, I feel as if I cannot help but write to you!

So I hope you enjoy reading *What Kind of Woman Is This?* It was for people just like you — special, unique, and one-of-a-kind — that this book was written.

— *Shoddy Chase*

Preface

"Mom, someone's at the door!" The young woman heard a child's voice call from within the house as she nervously waited on the doorstep.

"I've got it!" the mother's voice responded. Then the mother opened the front door and smiled kindly at the young woman she had been waiting for.

Greeting her with a warm embrace, the older woman said, "Hey, how are you? I'm so glad you're here!"

"Come in," she invited the young woman. "Please sit down and make yourself at home. I'll be right with you. By the way, you look great! A little jittery, maybe, but don't worry; everything will be fine. I have invested many hours for months into preparing for this day.

"The trip will take only a few days — and what a trip it will be!" she continued. "It's guaranteed to make a difference in your life or your money back. Is this all your stuff? You sure travel light. I know it's hard to pack when you don't know what to expect, so I always bring along extra in case someone forgets something. Okay, let's go!"

Such a kind hostess this woman was! Her friendly words surrounded the young woman like a cozy, warm blanket as

she stood there feeling frightened, excited, peaceful, and anxious — just one big bundle of emotions mixed with a deep desire to change.

I remember well the day I felt just like that young woman. Even more importantly, I remember the day when I came to the end of myself. In that lonely place, I realized that I needed to know Him in a deeper way.

Before that time, I was far too embarrassed to admit that I couldn't make it on my own. Reaching out to someone for help was worse than humbling; it made me feel stupid, frail, and frightened.

Looking back now, I can smile and acknowledge that my "end-of-myself" feelings would prove to be the beginning of everything good in my life.

I guess the greatest lesson I learned those many years ago was that I needed people. Certainly I needed the Lord, but I also needed someone to help show me the way. I had thought I knew the way, but I really didn't. I came to realize that I was never supposed to journey this life alone. I was not made to be *weak*, but I *was* made to be *dependent.*

Now here I am leading others to a higher place. I point them to that deeper place of dependence and need, that secret place where peace and purpose rule forever.

All that any of us are looking for is found on a particular mountain. I'm not talking about a Himalayan peak in Tibet or Nepal, but about Mount Moriah — the mountain of sacrifice and of praise. Long ago on that spiritual mountain, I discovered that the secret place is Christ.

The day I came to the end of myself so many years ago was a turning point in my life. I have never returned, at least not the same.

So now it's your turn! Are you ready for some things to change in *your* life so you can soar into clearer, brighter skies?

Too often this world's worries and doubts so dim God's light in our lives that even our faith seems faded and dull. But the Holy Ghost can do a work! No matter how cloudy the scenery is that we face in life, just one glimpse of God's glory and of our value in Him can change every shade of gray that surrounds us into the brilliant colors of the rainbow!

You see, as the Church, the Bride of Jesus Christ, we are a city in the process of being built. God describes that city as *"having the glory of God: and her light was like unto a stone most precious, even like a jasper stone, clear as crystal"* (Rev. 21:11 *KJV*). "Her light" refers to your light and my light — our ways, our wisdom, and our insight — that can shine like jewels because of Jesus, who is the glory of God.

But only when you start to truly see — that is, when God's truth is revealed to your heart concerning His work and your worth — can God's "great and precious promises" begin to transform the colors in your life that over the years may have grown so dim. I pray that this writing helps provide you with a glimpse of that great revelation so the drab greens in your world can turn to emerald and the dull reds can become rubies.

So let's see how one woman grew and changed until her life shone like a brilliant jasper stone. Perhaps by looking at her life, you and I can begin to begin to see "as clear as crystal" God's glory at work within our own lives as well.

Chapter One

The Mom, the King, and 'The Virtuous Woman'

*A*s I began writing this book about Proverbs 31, I debated as to whether or not I should include all thirty-one verses. The most famous part of Proverbs 31 starts with verse 10, which begins the description of "the Virtuous Woman." I have opted to dedicate most of my time and attention in this book to this very special woman, but I did want to give some acknowledgment to the first nine verses, since they are very powerful and relevant.

A Mother's Counsel to Her Son

The sobering words of counsel in these first nine verses are for any saint or sovereign. They are the words of a mother instructing her son, who also happens to be her

king. King Lemuel is repeating what his mother has taught him, so she in essence is the one speaking.

> **The words of King Lemuel, the utterance which his mother taught him:**
>
> **What, my son? And what, son of my womb? And what, son of my vows?**
>
> **Do not give your strength to women, nor your ways to that which destroys kings.**
>
> **It is not for kings, O Lemuel, it is not for kings to drink wine, nor for princes intoxicating drink;**
>
> **Lest they drink and forget the law, and pervert the justice of all the afflicted.**
>
> **Give strong drink to him who is perishing, and wine to those who are bitter of heart.**
>
> **Let him drink and forget his poverty, and remember his misery no more.**
>
> **Open your mouth for the speechless, in the cause of all who are appointed to die.**
>
> **Open your mouth, judge righteously, and plead the cause of the poor and needy.**
>
> **— Proverbs 31:1-9**

This passage of Scripture is clearly directed to a man of power and position. However, although the sobering words included in these verses are not specifically spoken to ordinary men, they pertain to all men.

This mother knows the foolishness that can make a man stumble and fall. So she reminds her son of the temptations that are capable of making the king of a nation weaken and forget why he is king — until he eventually falls victim to his own sin.

These nine verses waste no time; the speaker gets right to the point. Her son is a king; his time is of great value.

What she says is both concise and precise, and for that he is grateful. Her words will be easily remembered.

How interesting that before we find the description of a virtuous woman, we are provided the tools for a virtuous king — and a virtuous man!

Verses 3, 4, 5, and 8 bring "the prophecy" that this mother taught her son down to earth so all of us can clearly understand what she is saying. Let me paraphrase the words of King Lemuel's mother:

"My precious son, listen to me. I have vowed to instruct you. I have given you life, and with that gift of life I will also help lead you. Here are my words of wisdom to you: Protect your God-given anointing to lead a nation. Don't give your strength to loose women, nor your ways to the temptations that destroys kings. Stay away from wine and dirty deals. Open your mouth and judge righteously.

"I have just told you how to walk as a wise king. Now it's up to you to *be* a wise king."

Every man or woman in any capacity of leadership should read and reread this God-inspired, God-desired proclamation!

What a mother this woman must have been! Although perhaps a little dreamy in nature, she was nonetheless a woman of great pursuit. She obviously possessed a deep desire for her son to meet a woman who wore glory and grandeur like vestments. She longed to see her loving Lemuel snuggled up in the all-adoring affection of this special woman — the sought-after, soon-to-be-famous-to-all-generations *Proverbs 31 Woman*!

Looking for This Elusive Woman

Homosapiens around the globe are in pursuit of this paragon of virtue and beauty. Large segments of the male sector of society have gone wild over her, from the Christian community to the most secluded of all known religions. Even heathen men love this woman!

Men who don't even own a Bible (for example, the Iran Jayra tree people of Indonesia) will go purchase one just to read the famous phraseology found in the twentieth book of "the most Holy Book," also known as the book of Proverbs.

Now for those of you not familiar with the Bible, a *proverb* as defined in the *Merriam Webster Dictionary* is "a pithy (brief and to the point), popular saying."[1] Some may argue that the proverbs in this book of the Bible are *not* popular truths. But we will see...

In the book of Proverbs, we find that the key word is *wisdom*. The definition of wisdom is "the ability to live life skillfully."[2] There's no argument that wisdom is something we could all use more of. We all need more skill in living successfully on this big ball of clay!

In fact, "Learning How *Not* To Get Stuck in the Mud in Our Journey Through Life" should be a required college course! Certainly it's an undertaking we should all diligently pursue.

The Greek title for Proverbs is *Paroimiai Salomontos*.[3] (It sounds like something I ordered last week at Gourmet Café!) The Latin title *Liber Proverbiorum*, meaning "Book

of Proverbs," denotes the way that proverbs concentrate many words into a few.[4]

"Many words into a few." That sounds good. Trimming the fat off some of our corpulent conversation wouldn't hurt us at all!

So wisdom that promotes precision, accurate timing in life, correct priorities, and the flow of life's seasons — these are some of the hallmarks of Proverbs. In fact, the rabbinical writings call Proverbs *Sepher Hokhmah*, the "Book of Wisdom."[5]

The first thirty chapters of this divinely inspired book I leave to you to study in private. But let's put at least one chapter — Chapter 31 — of this "Book of Wisdom" under the microscope. As we scrutinize it, the wisdom hidden within its verses will help us "live life skillfully" during our sojourn on this earth.

So come with me, and let's find out what all males in the Milky Way galaxy already know: There is someone whom all women are supposed to emulate — none other, of course, than the Proverbs 31 woman. We'll discover why so many (especially those with the XY chromosomal make-up!) find this particular portion of Scripture to be the most divinely inspiring of the entire written Word of God!

What a Gal She Must Have Been!

It's interesting to note that in the Old Testament alone, there are 39 books to choose from, 929 chapters to fall in love with, and 23,214 verses to quote.[6] Yet what passage of Scripture do we women hear about all the time? The chapter

about the famed, the one and only, Proverbs 31 woman, of course!

This woman was (and I stress the word *was*) the greatest, most educated, and most powerful woman on the face of the earth at the time. Even still today her words are echoed.

Just take a moment to listen carefully. Go ahead — go outside, cup your hand gently behind your ear, and listen. Quiet now...do you hear it? Just wait a moment, and you will.

There it is! Some man somewhere is out in his front yard on a quiet evening, imitating a wolf howling at the moon as he quotes Proverbs 31!

The oracle who wrote of this woman succeeded in carving into the gray matter of man twenty-two verses of a poem that, until the sun rises no more, will forever compel women to live up to her high standard. This prestigious woman (or this pesky woman, however you look at it!) has changed forever the way the world looks at the female gender.

Who Can Find This Virtuous Women?
(She's Closer Than You Think!)

Excuse me now for a moment, dear reader, I want to address King Lemuel.

Just one thing, Lemuel — how old were you when dear ol' Mommy filled your cranial cavity with all these marvels of motherhood? Could this incredible woman that Mom talked about just be make believe? Or could this actually be

a real story about a real woman who lives in a real world and desires to be a real woman of God?

You don't know? Well, let me ask you this, Lemuel: Is it possible that your mom never wanted you to marry? Now, don't look so shocked, as if you hadn't thought of this before. How can I be so bold as to say such a thing? Well, for starters, the beginning of her "Seminar for Ensured Sainthood" states the question clear and simple: *"Who can find a virtuous woman?..."* (v. 10). Is the standard so high that she thought you would never find the woman she dreamed up?

"Who can find a virtuous woman?" What if the answer is "No one"?

I'm trying to make you understand, Lemuel, that this perfect package does not exist. Face it, Pal. Look around out there. Have you met her yet? Just what I thought — no, you haven't. Well, join the masses of dejected and heavy-hearted men in the valley of "We Told You, But You Wouldn't Listen."

Excuse me, Lemuel, but you needed to hear that grim and possibly earth-shattering news.

This veritable masterpiece of feminine virtue does not exist — not the way you think! But another masterpiece does. And maybe you have just never had an eye for art. Hang in there; we can change that.

So who *can* find this woman? It depends on what kind of woman we are talking about. You see, a queer sort of search is underway among the throngs of men to find that perfect "10." With hope in their hearts and the words of Lemuel's mother ever before them, these men pursue what

I believe to be a mystical illusion. Well, I'm here to wake them up.

To these men, I say, "You have been like thirsty men in a desert, chasing a mirage — a blurry, undefined Hollywood hoax of what a true woman is. Now, personally, I do believe the virtuous woman can be found. She does exists, and she can exist in every woman.

"This true woman is out there, men, and she's everything you need and desire. Her package might be wrapped differently than you thought, but the contents will knock your socks off!"

Let the Voice of God Ring Out!

Let's pause now for a moment to consider the three communicators in the Old Testament who spoke on behalf of God: The priests imparted the Law; the prophets communicated divine messages and visions; and the sages gave counsel to the people, providing practical application to specific problems. (I guess we can safely say that sage does add a certain flavor and spice to things, making the mundane more pleasant!)

Oh, my, I only told you about *three* communicators who spoke on behalf of God. I forgot about mothers — women in general, for that matter — such as, of course, Lemuel's mom.

The Perils of P-A-L-A-C-E *Life*

Do keep in mind that this passage of Scripture is a poem. Like most poetry, it's a bit glassy and far away, with

a mystical haze hanging over the magic it portrays. Now let's study this acrostic of twenty-two verses.

First, what makes it an acrostic? Starting in verse 10, each verse through 31 begins with a different Hebrew letter according to the order of the Hebrew alphabet.[7] So if you're ready now, let's analyze this scriptural poem.

The word *analyze* means "to separate into parts or basic principles so as to determine the nature of the whole; to examine methodically."[8]

Analyze? Yes that's right. Lemuel, we will analyze — separate into basic parts or principles — this enigma and be beautified by its compelling declarations.

Please, Lemuel, indulge me once more. I promise that after this I'll be good. But it's about your mother again. I'm sure she was a fine and splendid person of the palace, but — that's my point. The palace!

Yes, Lemuel, the P-A-L-A-C-E.

May I ask where your mom located this "relative of Zeus"-like goddess? If I am not mistaken, palace duties did not include such an inventory of activities as this incredible woman engaged in.

So where did Momma find her? Or did she? Or does this Proverbs 31 woman potentially reside in every woman? Is she someone a man *finds* or someone a woman *becomes?* That is what we will see.

I Think We Get the Message

The Proverbs 31 woman has been the focus of many a sermon. Lecterns throughout the civilized world have taken beatings from red-faced, yelling, perspiring preachers who want to make sure we females get the point.

Personally, I think we get the message — loud and clear! Now, don't get me wrong. I love to listen to red-faced, yelling, perspiring preachers expound on Proverbs 31.

The truth is, I adore Proverbs 31. I'm willing to die trying to live up to all it conveys.

But the question remains: Can no one find a virtuous woman? Did they all die somewhere between verses 13 and 31? We're going to find out, not only for the sake of Lemuel and all those throngs of men, but for those of us of the female gender as well. As women, we need to know: Since it's a sure bet that we can't be perfect, is it possible to live up to the example set for us by this wonder woman of Proverbs 31?

Chapter Two

Let's Begin Our Expedition

Who can find a virtuous wife? For her worth is far above rubies.

The heart of her husband safely trusts her; so he will have no lack of gain.

She does him good and not evil all the days of her life.

— Proverbs 31:10-12

We find out in these verses that this awe-inspiring "better half" possesses something far greater than the value of rubies; she has *virtue.* She is a virtuous woman. And because she is a virtuous woman, she certainly will be a virtuous wife, because spouses bring into their marriages who they are.

This virtuous woman possesses a valiant spirit; she is both brave and bold. She is a potent force. Her standard is high, but her heart is humble. Do not ask her to

compromise her ethics; you will only shame yourself. And because of this virtue, she has a value far above rubies.

So far, no problem. I can live with verses 10, 11, and 12 — they're great!

The Heart of It All

Because of the virtue this woman possesses, she holds within her power the heart of another person. That is a power not to be taken lightly, dear reader. Holding the heart of another is sacred and precious. It is also very precarious, because the ability to inflict great hurt is ever so near.

But this woman's husband does not fear; in fact, he "safely trusts her." That's a trust to cherish. It is no ordinary trust. It requires no questions, no sleepless nights wondering what she will do in strange situations. He *knows* how she will handle life because she is virtuous. Therefore, the husband feels safe.

Worth Is the Womb Where Self-Esteem Is Born

Let's backtrack for a moment. There's a word in verse 10 that touches us all, a word that shouldn't be read so quickly nor easily dismissed. That word is *worth.* I zoomed past it earlier, but now let's zoom in on it.

Verse 10 says that *"…her worth is FAR ABOVE…."* Here we are told that this woman's value is highly esteemed. Most of the time we read this passage of Scripture and remember the part that says, *"The heart of her husband safely trusts*

her..." (v.11). But as we read further, let's remember the worth of this woman. It's above earthly substance of any kind.

Virtue — how true and regal a treasure! Nothing outshines its worth, not even a costly jewel. The worth of a virtuous woman is more dazzling and exquisite than a rare and precious ruby.

Yet virtue is sought after by so few. I'm saddened by the knowledge that rubies and other precious natural treasures are desired and sought after by more people than is an increase in virtue. Maybe I'm wrong. I hope so, but the state of this world would argue otherwise.

A morally good person is salt and light in any place he finds himself. Personally, the more good I do on this earth, the more I realize a worth residing within me that goes beyond my own confidence or human dignity. It is a heavenly worth — how *God* sees me — that I am perceiving.

You see, there is a natural worth that I understand and feel as a mom, and that is good. There is a worth a father feels, and that is also good. Yet outside anything we can produce that is deemed worthy in the natural, there is a divine degree of worth that each of us can stand in, simply because we were born by the foreordained plan of God. We are alive; therefore, we have value.

How glorious it is to exist as a human designed to fulfill a divine destiny! I find worth in this one fact: that *I am here*.

Being able to humbly acknowledge that there is something wonderful about you is one of the sure foundations on which to build your life. You see, *worth is the womb in which self-esteem is born.*

This worth of mine keeps me safe when all else fails. My sense of value and worth is my inner cloak that safely covers my emotions.

No matter what happens, I know I am somebody! Not only did Someone great fashion me, I am personally known by the Designer! (In the natural, I normally don't spend the money needed to purchase signature brands. But I smile, knowing that in God's eyes, I *am* a signature brand!)

He is the Great I Am, and I am a child of the Great I Am. So who does that make me? I would dare to answer: Someone who is pretty darn important!

He Trusts, and She Does Him Right
(or 'She's Got His Whole World in Her Hands')

The heart of her husband safely trusts her; so he will have no lack of gain.

— Proverbs 31:11

No fear exists in this relationship between husband and wife. Only serenity and trust is allowed. And where does this trusts come from? It's embedded in understanding. Husband, if you want your wife to do you right, then safely trust her.

I know it is not as easy to trust as I make it sound, but every journey must have a starting point. We must push off from port in our marriage without negative or critical comments or putdowns stowing away on board. Otherwise, our relationship with our spouse will end up in the noisy, hot, and grimy engine room — a place of great emotional anguish, of intensity and not intimacy.

Our relationships should live in the upper decks, where the cool air refreshes life and love, where abundance envelopes us and fine dining is enjoyed.

Though You've Been Hurt — Keep Trusting

As the world winds down and we approach the final days, a curtain of chaos is drawn, and we see the demise of much good — including trust.

Trusting people is often difficult because we've been disillusioned so many times. And sadly, it sometimes seems that trusting God is difficult as well. One has cast its shadow on the other, causing the brightness of trusting to be dimmed.

How can any relationship last without trust, especially the marital relationship? It cannot. When the life source has been cut off, death is inevitable.

Thank God, we see in Proverbs 31 a man who knows how to keep alive the love he has vowed to always give his wife: He does it by trusting her.

Proverbs 31:11 goes on to say that because the woman's husband safely trusts her, *"...he will have no lack of gain."* The couple's agreement is strong; therefore, no lack lives with them. Where there is trust, there is no lack.

The couple dreams as one, lives as one, and earns as one. Yet there is no loss of personal identity. Standing as a "me" and living as a "we" is the way marriage is supposed to work. In this kind of home, there is agreement. There is unity.

The force of unity has enough power in itself to build cities and tear down kingdoms. It is an invisible power, but its fruit can be seen. At times you can actually feel this force called unity when it is in operation, and you can sense the vacuum when it is absent.

And what about this Proverbs 31 couple? Their marriage is a powerful union of two "me's" into a one "we," just as God intended. And because of their unity and mutual trust, there is no lack of gain.

She Does Her Man Good

The Bible also says that *"she does him good and not evil all the days of her life"* (Prov. 31:12). She does her man good. What an achievement! Such a courageous venture this woman has undertaken — a lifetime walk, risking all for the sake of love.

This almost musical prelude to the poetic description of this virtuous woman is pure and pleasant and actually holds all the other verses in balance. Before we read about all the running around and domestic doings of this amazing woman, we find out that she takes care of her man. This responsibility is anything but dull. The woman understands that life has priorities, and her number-one priority after God is the man she has married.

"She does him good." This woman knows that if things are not right at home, everything feels awkward. It's as if the heart and emotions cannot keep pace with life.

"She does him good." She makes all things within the home flow like a restful stream. The rush and hectic activity of life can't disturb those deep waters of peace. Despite

it all, home life seems to move on with ease. An abiding sense of comfort assures each family member that all is fine; all is peaceful; there is love in this home.

"She does him good." She honors and cherishes her relationship with her husband. Before her busy day begins, she always finds time to consider this man who trusts her in such a precious way.

"She does him good." That *good* is what makes her different from the harsh world she sees. With the words she speaks and the love she shows, this woman knows how life works: "If I give and love, if I care and bless, God will take care of my needs."

She understands a secret shared only by those with pure hearts: "My life will reflect my soul, and all that I do today will be a part of me tomorrow. I will snuggle up in the cozy, loving home I have created. The comfort of friends and the closeness of family will be my warmth in a world of winters."

Like an artist with a brush or a chisel in the hand of a sculptor, so is a woman who has this vision for her family: "I will design a work of art, and all who see it will be silenced one breathless moment by its strength. This treasure will be the love *that* my husband and I share and the life that we've made together."

we make

Chapter Three

Don't Give Me No Flack —
Just Plenty of Flax, Please!

She seeks wool and flax, and willingly works with her hands.

— Proverbs 31:13

*I*n Bible times, you couldn't get any better than wool and flax. Back then, wool and flax were the big thing! Of course, silk outclassed wool and flax, but that was definitely a costly little worm excretion not all could afford!

However, money is not the issue in this verse about the virtuous woman. Silk wasn't around yet; it was brought into Israel about 325 B.C. reaching the Bible lands after the conquest of Alexander the Great.[9] (I knew you were wondering about that!)

Anyway, Sheshi and Meshi are in a different "dinero dimension," so let's just stick with the materials at hand. (If you were perplexed, "Sheshi" and "Meshi" are the Hebrew names for silk,[10] not the dog and cat of the late Liberace, God rest his soul!)

Shopping Is Sanctioned by the Word!

Now again I quote: *"She seeks wool and flax...."* I think we're on to something here. This woman seeks *wool* and *flax*. Not cotton, mind you. Back then, cotton was *not* the "fabric of our lives." Oh, yes, Bible buddy, this virtuous lady likes the name brands — or at least the highest quality she can afford.

Can you imagine a modern wife waking one fine morning and saying, "Dear, sweet husband, today I will set out to seek wool and flax"?

The husband most likely would roll his eyes and curl his lips in strange contortions, mumbling the words, "Oh, gee...well, go have fun."

God, the Mall, and Me

If you are one of my female readers, do you realize the information I have just imparted? This verse about wool and flax and the seeking thereof could be your ticket to the mall!

(Arise, shine, for your light has come! Grab your flashlight and come on, because "Midnight Madness" is about to begin!)

Wool was one of the chief materials for dress in the Bible days. The economy of Bible lands relied heavily on wool. Let's not ignore the fact that those sheep were sheared — and for what? For nothing? No, no, a thousand times, no!

Oh, friend in fashion, my alter ego, listen to me. I appeal to the apparel side of all. I hereby state that it is your moral and civil obligation to seek wool and flax!

Our economy depends upon the faithful shopper who realizes the spiritual responsibility of spending money. "Ewe" owe it to yourself and all of mankind to go buy a little sheep skin! (Okay, I admit that I'm getting a little carried away. Visions of shopping all day can do that to me!)

The way I look at it, someone has to do the shopping in the family. I guess I will be the one — and willingly at that!

A willing consumer is a happy consumer. We can choose to be happy as we go forth into the hustle and bustle of life to shop. It can actually be fun to search among the wool and flax, shoving our way through crowds to get to every sale just so little Johnny can have a new shirt.

Proverbs 31:13 also says the virtuous woman *"... willingly works with her hands."* She is not a clutterbug; she gets what she needs, and she needs what she gets. She returns home from shopping ready to work some more. Her hands never seem to stop working. I believe she likes it that way.

You know, it's not easy to schedule my life around the mall, but with God's help, I'll do it. In fact, great spiritual moments have happened for me at the mall. Reminisce with me a moment.

I remember one time I had a vision while buying underwear for my husband. It was during a "Fruit of the Loom Sale" in mid-October. His briefs were all worn out due to the summer heat. The elastic had just disappeared! Truly it was a mystery that now awaits production on the "X Files."

All that remained was bits of cloth hanging loosely around my husband's belly — a truly funny sight. But I got tired of him constantly complaining to me that every other husband he knew had nice, new underwear. (How would he know what kind of underwear other husbands wore, anyway?)

So I bundled up and took off for the mall. As I picked up a package of briefs, I saw a flash of light suddenly illuminate the Fruit of the Loom trademark logo. As I looked more closely, it appeared that the beautifully clustered fruit was laughing, just like a happy family!

To me, the message was simple: Although we are different, we are in one big, happy family — God's family. I was so moved, I wept for days after that. (I'm sure you will, too, after reading about this vision!)

On escalators, I've received sermons about Heaven and hell. In the giant malls, I've realized afresh how great our God is, "His wonders to perform"!

Flax, Fabulous Flax

Flax is a precious and versatile material that was even more important than wool in Bible times. It's made from the flax plant, the woody stem of which also furnishes fiber

for fine linen. You see, flax can be made coarse and thick or very fine and delicate.

Fine linen made a fashion statement back then and was used by those of position and wealth. This woman in Proverbs 31 is starting to look better and getting easier to understand all the time. *Ladies!* She's speaking our language!

Bring In Those Merchant Ships!

My husband can no longer say anything about how I wreak havoc on the local shops, assault the malls, or drain his wallet. I'm like a smart missile; I target my sale and attack. If the "Mr." wails and whines, I take him to Proverbs 31, and with the help of "Mr. Pointer," I lead him to verse 14 for enlightenment!

She is like the merchant ships, she brings her food from afar.

— Proverbs 31:14

Can you fathom this? This special woman's shopping spree is not compared to one ship. *Oh, no!* She needs *ships,* plural! Verse 14 also says that *"...she brings her food from afar."* (In other words, she likes the imported stuff!)

This lady, my heroine, gets up while it's still dark out. I can see her now. For weeks now, she's been planning this shopping trip. And now, before her husband even wakes up, she's out of that house! She's a woman with a mission. Okay, okay, I should adjust my story a little bit. That's not exactly how the story goes. This virtuous woman does make breakfast; *then* she toddles on out!

Chapter Four

Maids, Wonderful Maids!

She also rises while it is yet night, and provides food for her household, and a portion for her maidservants.

— Proverbs 31:15

*L*et me now echo one of the greatest statements I have ever read. This wonder woman whom everyone looks up to *"... provides food for her household, and a portion for HER MAIDSERVANTS."*

Is that terrific or what? It says maidservants. Did you get that? No wonder the lady can run around and be involved in every business deal in town — she has maids!

I love it. I always knew that it was biblical to have servants!

Be a Woman of the Word — Get a Maid!

Seriously, though, both in ancient and in modern Middle Eastern culture, it is common to have hired help.

In this modern world, Americans are actually on the primitive end of the spectrum regarding the practice of hiring "helpers." (That's what the profession is called in the Philippines, where I live and minister with my family.)

Around the globe in more countries than I can count, families have either an aunt, a grandmother, or some other relative living with them, aiding and assisting in the art of staying alive.

You see, life at times is like running up a sand dune: gritty and painful. And sometimes you can run for what seems to be a very long time, only to look behind and see to your utter shock that you've hardly gained any ground! Other times, a lot of time and energy is required just to retake *lost* ground.

For millions of women (including myself!), the thought of running up those sand dunes alone — in other words, *doing it all* without any help — is enough to cause a sudden outbreak of eczema. As the old Beatle song goes, "Help! I need somebody! Help! Not just anybody. Help! You know, I need someone!" Yes, we do need someone — equipped with a toilet brush and a vacuum cleaner!

It's Time To Get Back to the Bible

I have endeavored to be a woman of the Word ever since I got born again way back at the turn of the century

(okay, maybe it hasn't been quite *that* long!). Being a devout woman of the Word means that I should embrace the sacred writings in every area of my life.

Well, then, if hubby wants his wife to be like the Proverbs 31 paragon of virtue, then I want a maid. It is purely scriptural. God has ordained it. (Do I hear an *"Amen?"*)

No Maid? Check Out Your Kids!

If you cannot afford a maid, I suggest that you use your children. I mean, why is it that kids these days do "diddly-squat," barely lifting a finger around the house to help? Do they eat there, sleep there, and shower there?

The house that your family lives in is a home, not a hotel; a kitchen, not a mission; a bedroom, not a shelter. It is also not a hostel for the backpacking tourist. I think there should be some kind of law that forces kids, primarily American children, to first mow their own lawn and then go mow some elderly person's lawn — for *free*! Then they could take out the trash for the entire neighborhood and work every other Saturday doing community service just for good measure!

Don't tell me about your rights, you darling little slug-gard who has never observed the ants. You are a child in need of being trained in the way you should go. You have not yet earned any rights.

So whether it's our kids, our husband, or one of those wonderful maids, just remember one thing: It's God's desire that we have help around the home as we run up those sand dunes of life!

Chapter Five

Is There Nothing She Can't Do?

She considers the field and buys it; from her profits she plants a vineyard.

— Proverbs 31:16

ll right, Sherlock, are you seeing what I'm seeing? This woman whom we adore really has it all together. Notice verse 16. Does she simply go shopping with some friends? No way! She feeds the man of the house and the little ones, and then she goes and buys a field! (Of course, she buys a field. Don't all woman everywhere have that on their "to do list"?)

This wonderful creature, the famous Proverbs 31 woman — the one we are to be just like — went out and bought a field. The book says she considered it and then bought it. She never even went home and discussed the matter with "you-know-who."

You won't hear me complaining about being old-fashioned. I like old-fashioned — Old Testament style, that is! Ah, yes, the good ol' days!

I want to know where the money came from for this woman to buy that field. You know, fields aren't cheap! Verse 15 gives me my answer: *"She also rises while it is yet night...."* Oh, I get it. While *he* snores, *she* is snooping around for his hidden stash!

No, I'm just kidding. This resourceful wife was probably just thrifty with the grocery money. She saved a denarius here and there, and before she knew it, she had what she needed to buy a field! We are reading a description of one of the most competent, skilled, shrewd, and contriving mothers any of us would ever want to meet!

Hang on to your beeper, because this business transaction is not yet fully executed. Proverbs 31:16 says that after this woman buys the field, she *sells* it!

Wow, do you believe this extraordinary lady's business sense? And even more unbelievable is the fact that husbands all over the world want *us* to be like this woman! Are they sure? Are you really ready, men?

I'm sitting here shaking my head in total amazement. This many-sided saint is now a real-estate broker. Oh, the wonders of the Word of God. I never realized such nuggets were nestled within its pages!

Not only does this woman sell the field she bought, but *"...from her profits she plants a vineyard"* (Prov. 31:16)! You know, I have heard it said, "The farmer went forth and plowed and planted and weeded and harvested (all in the same day); then he died from exposure." The message is

clear; a person can't do everything in one day. But that doesn't seem to apply to this woman — she can do no wrong!

Now, we all realize that farming is a skill. It requires knowledge that is gained through years of learning, training, and experimenting in *agriculture*, which is the science, art, and business of cultivating the soil, producing crops, and raising livestock. So now we find out our wonder woman, who not only teaches on CNN Business Asia, is also an agriculturist!

I ask you — how can this woman do these spectacular feats? And where does she get her energy?

Chapter Six

She Girds Herself With Strength

She girds herself with strength, and strengthens her arms.

— Proverbs 31:17

he verb *to gird* means "to prepare oneself for action."[11] That's the crucial point here. Preparing herself for action, this woman *girds* herself with strength.

Here are some other definitions of *to gird*:[12] 1) to encircle or bind with a belt or band; 2) to surround; endorse; hem in; 3) to prepare oneself for action; brace; 4) to equip or invest, as with power or strength.

Now I see what's going on. Behind the mystery of all that is written about the virtuous woman, here in this verse her secret — if it ever was a secret — is shared. Everything

we will learn about her both in previous and future verses finds its lifeline and link to verse 17.

If a person is successful to any degree in his or her endeavors, you can know there has been some girding going on. This woman's "inner gird beam" holds up all her endeavors, and it's evident to all.

How To Gird

One of the ways I gird myself with inner strength is through those stolen moments called "quiet times." Alone with myself, I sip on coffee and solitude. I take time to think, or I go out in the yard and gaze at my surroundings. I know the strength given to the one who will be still and wait before the Lord. I prepare myself for action by being still.

Another way I gird myself is through worship. How can a Christian breathe freely without praising God? The Lord said it to me this way: "Like an angel with a broken wing, so are Christians who refuse to sing." They simply will not be able to fly.

If I gird my inner life, my outer life will mirror the time I have invested. So I surround and encircle my heart and emotions with God's strength, because I am well aware of the spiritual battlefield I walk through every day. I realize there are mines placed by the enemy just waiting for me to step on them to my destruction.

But, thank God, because I've not carelessly approached life — I am girded! I'm guarded. I have girded myself with God's Word and His ways. Obedience to Him is the girder,

the principal beam, that holds up my life and the life of my family.

God takes care of me and guides me. I have waited upon the Lord, and He has surely renewed my staggering strength. Arms that normally might want to hang heavy and low cannot help but be lifted in joy, for God is the strength of my life!

Of course this virtuous woman girds herself with strength, for she is wise. She isn't depending on her own human strength either. She draws on a power that belongs to the Lord. He freely portions out this strength according to a person's heart devotion to Him.

So if you are weary and worn out, I believe you are a candidate for a divine power surge. Get on your knees, lift up your arms, start to sing, and start to pray. Start loving on God, and you will automatically gird yourself with strength!

The Shape You Find Yourself in Is Really Up to You

There is a down-to-earth side to this heavenly woman as well. Besides girding herself with spiritual strength, she also "strengthens her arms."

You know, a little exercise does wonders for the down-cast soul. A small change in diet, such as less junk food and an occasional apple, will brighten your eyes and your skin, and make you feel more than good.

Notice also that this woman is not a wimp. It says *she* strengthens her arms. She isn't looking for someone else to

get her in shape, spiritually *or* physically. Others can help, but that is about all they can do.

I wholeheartedly try to encourage people through my preaching, my poetry, or my teaching to "strengthen their own arms." Every song I sing and every scripture I speak in essence shows how to gird oneself.

Sadly, I feel so limited. I hate that aspect of the ministry, because I know that if I could only do the girding for the person I am ministering to, I would see a new life emerge. But I cannot live my passion nor conviction through another. We all must learn to "strengthen our own arms."

Mentors are no doubt needed as examples for us to follow. As we learn from their victories and the mistakes they made along the way, we are able to go forward with less scars that need healing, and not nearly as much time is wasted.

But when it is all said and done, you must choose your destiny. You must heed Heaven's voice. You will stand before the Lord on that great and mighty day by yourself. You will stand before Him alone.

And how strong your arms are on that day will be totally up to you.

Chapter Seven

She Works and Works — and Works!

She perceives that her merchandise is good, and her lamp does not go out by night.

She stretches out her hands to the distaff, and her hand holds the spindle.

— Proverbs 31:18,19

*T*his magnificent mother, although aging rapidly (lack of sleep will do that to you!), was schooled in all manner of materials and fabrics. I read that when she was three years of age, her first attempt at a tapestry proved rewarding.

At age four, she made a quilt that people still talk about.

At age seven, she taught a few kids in the neighborhood in detail about the different types of fibers. She also

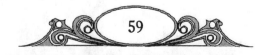

taught distaff spinning, weaving, tanning, and embroidering.

Well, that was the beginning. Even today, some of those "kids" still work in this woman's companies.

The Lady Works!

According to verse 18, she has a keen sense of what is marketable — what will sell and what will never appeal to the consumer she has targeted. She is the first strategist in her neck of the woods with a twenty-four-hour factory. Not only did her controversial "The Girdle Company" make the papers, but "The Weaving Woman" is a highly successful business as well. "The Woof and Warp" opens next year.

Brainstorming for her next specialty shop, designed to make priestly garments and tabernacle needs, has recently intensified. She will call the new shop "Threads of Mercy."

This lady is industrious, to say the least. She possesses the attributes of a corporate tycoon, yet has the heart and soul of Florence Nightingale. The word *lazy* is not in her vocabulary.

Back in her grade-school days, she blacked out during a spelling bee when the word *lazy* was given to her to spell. Her classmates all knew then that this girl was *different*! Any word referring to a "couch potato" type of human, such as *slob* or *sluggard*, would also produce severe reactions.

Classmates also learned early about the dreaded "L" words: *lethargic, lackadaisical, languid, languorous,* and *list-less.* She made her friends learn those words, so they would

not *be* those words. She also made sure that *she* was not any of them, and at that she most triumphantly succeeded.

This woman works! End of sentence, but the beginning of her story. What a great thing for someone to say about another person. It's not a bad legacy to leave behind in a world where plenty of "L" people loiter about. *She works.*

I can read your mind. You're thinking, *So what? I work too. That really isn't earth-shattering news.* Well, friend, it must be important news because it made the pages of the Bible!

You see, so few *really* work. Many people punch a time clock. Thousands go somewhere and spend hours doing what will eventually be called *their life.* But in reality, so few really work with zest and heartfelt passion.

One day I was thumbing through a *Reader's Digest* when I came upon an article that dealt with high-paid, well-liked executives (as you know, the two don't necessarily go together). The executives all answered an interviewer's questions — questions that seemed quite ordinary.

For instance, they were asked, "What is your secret to success?" One response seemed to leap off the pages when I read it: "I never had a job I didn't like." In other words, this particular person fulfilled the responsibilities of every job he ever had with his whole heart. That is a great attitude! That's a winner's attitude. That kind of disposition will cause every area of a person's life to be full, happy, and exciting.

It really peeves me when I hear that a business owner's child grew up and became the boss — *unless he or she truly had the heart and soul to take the helm.* If the child

was reared in riches without responsibility, a self-centered brat emerges instead of a person who has learned compassion and responsibility through some kind of hands-on work. In this case, company employees will never know the security of a leader, only the tantrums of a child they have to call "Boss."

How many people have grown up lacking the skills it takes to make decisions? How many have never been taught the skill of how to ponder and plan? The ability to achieve is taught by example. Then again, sometimes the work itself becomes the teacher.

Have you ever been around someone who grunts and barks out orders when, in your heart, you know that same person has never done the task he or she is demanding of you? That kind of situation can really test those "honor" and "submit" verses we all love so dearly!

Be an Adult – Learn To Hold the Spindle

Proverbs 31:19 says, *"She stretches out her hands to the distaff, and HER HAND HOLDS THE SPINDLE."* The Word of God does *not* say she stretches out her hand to her staff, pointing and provoking. If the "weaving wonder" is around the plant for the day, you can bet she is working as well as watching. She stretches out her hands to *work.*

I love to work. I started working at an early age. I don't recommend it, but at the same time, I don't regret it.

When I was twelve years old, I started working at a pizza restaurant located near to our house. I worked the register

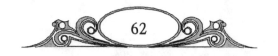

for a while and then graduated to the honorable position of a waitress. They even let me serve beer. (We were not a Christian family at the time, so pouring beer at the age of twelve was no big deal.)

I received no salary because of my age, but I did make tips, and that was fine with me. Not only did I like making money, but the work in itself was rewarding. I developed a sense of honor, and in my twelve-year-old mind, I felt rather grown up. Later I found out I *was* rather grown up for my age, at least within the world of those who worked.

You see, I became a contributor. I felt that because I worked, I had become a person who could actually make a difference.

Living in 'Grown-Up' Land

What a fascinating journey to embark on — the transition from being a receiver and a taker to one who relinquishes and gives, from a child who has always been taken care of to a "real" member of society, capable and required to help take care for others. Many adults, sad to say, have not crossed over that chasm, which is the very thing that separates them from children.

But we can easily walk the isthmus into "Grown-Up Land" when we learn how to live by "holding the spindle."

So look at your hands. Tell me, what do you see? What do those hands of yours hold? What do they touch? What your hands have done tells a story about who you are. If they've never held the spindle, then you've never crossed the chasm.

Teach Them Early To Hold the Spindle

Speaking of children — we all know the attitude that says, "Gimme, gimme, and gimme some more." That is the song all children know; they even hum it in the womb. Then upon delivery, they spread it through mental telepathy to every child in the nursery!

Children of every race, creed, and color have one thing in common — their *nature*! They are all alike. Have you noticed that yet? It's an incredible conspiracy. All four-year-old boys have their fingers stuck up their noses, and all kids, until taught differently, are selfish and greedy!

We parents are left trying to understand and find a way to laugh through those greedy and embarrassing moments. You know the moments I mean. For instance, your family is attending a family reunion, and relatives from near and far are getting reintroduced to each other. All is well until your little one decides to *beg.* Or maybe he decides to point and laugh, mocking the bloodline he has never even *seen* or *met* before!

I'm talking about those times when you watch your child act as if he or she was raised in the zoo. You try to convince yourself that this is not your child; this *cannot* be your child. But deep inside, you know you're the owner.

Well, what's a parent to do? *R-e-l-a-x.*

Good, hard work will cure children (and all the rest of us too!) of the "gimme, gimmies." So if your child is too young to hold the spindle, start with the pacifier!

I don't recommend making children work while they are still learning to walk, mind you. But, in balance, work gives a child a "pinnacle point of view" that will affect his or her entire outlook on life.

Never Trust a Lazy Man

You see, if you are a lazy person, you observe life from a low-life, lazy perspective. You have a distant look in your eye, non-caring and critical.

Every problem will seem hard to solve, because every problem (according to those unacquainted with work) is the fault of everybody else. The "Blame Game" is practiced and rehearsed like a well-loved anthem.

On the other hand, a calloused hand teaches the heart what it means to sweat, hope, dream, and respect. Spiritual things come easier to a person who works and sees the rewards of toil.

However, let's not get ridiculous — too much toil isn't good either. Remember, our lady of non-leisure does have a few maids.

But the truth is, honest, hard work does reflect back on the soul. That's why you should never trust a lazy person. If his body does nothing, can you imagine what his thought patterns are like? A little scary to contemplate, don't you think? The frontal lobe of his brain probably has a "For Rent" sign hanging on it!

Dream — But Don't Go To Sleep

Now back to this almost-worshipped woman that we've read so much about. When I slow down and think about it, I realize how hard-working she must have been.

We have peeped into her private world. We have been allowed to follow along, watching her every move. While she shopped, we have observed her bargaining and bartering.

We certainly know how creative she is. We've learned all about her companies; she's taught us free of charge. We have gathered so much knowledge from her. I feel forever indebted. All this wealth of insight is like priceless jewels.

She doesn't offer you any flowery or fancy words. There is no easy street map to purchase. No secret tunnels. No shortcuts to success.

But as with Dorothy in the Land of Oz, there is a path to follow, a few friends to help you, a forest of frustration and fear to conquer, and plenty of demons to denounce. Then right before you reach your Emerald City — the dream God has planted in your heart — something will for sure try to lull you to sleep. That's when it's so important to hold on to your dream!

Tears and Discouragement: Part of the Payment (Not the Penalty) For Making Dreams Come True

As we consider the lives of those who achieve and enjoy fulfilled lives, we get a panoramic view of what it

means to be a dreamer. We begin to learn how to keep our dreams alive.

From Dorothy and from our main character, the Proverbs 31 woman, we learn how to keep on walking even when weary toward the brightness of our dream — that ever-present goal which beckons us. And we might even find our way back home as we keep walking. But if we don't follow the path that lies before us to our dream, we will be left lost and lonely, unable to fulfill our destiny.

So this Proverbs 31 woman of excellence is teaching us how to walk in faith and have a vision for our lives. And it all starts with good, hard work.

"Her lamp doesn't go out by night." You see, to speak about our great plans for the future, better known as dreams, comes easy. It's organizing them and agonizing over them and carrying them out that at times makes *dreaming* more like a *nightmare* than an answer to prayer.

Discouragement and tears wash away many dreams. The dreamer, tired of the struggle, neatly puts away his or her spirit of purpose. When that happens, destiny hangs its head.

Dreams Cost

Not realizing that a dream costs something, people often take offense at its brutal payment plan. Dreams demand strength and will not survive without tenacity. Dreams devour our time and attention. In fact, time and attention are a dream's nerve center, purpose is its breath, and dedication is its heart, pumping life into every part of the dream.

Dreams that are never hugged nor lived, but instead are left alone, become abandoned. Those discarded as "could-have-been" dreams cost us all. The world becomes a little heavier in heart, for it knows another dream has just died.

"Her lamp doesn't go out by night." Even at those "midnight hours" of her life, this woman of excellence keeps the flames of her future burning bright. In the sad and confusing times, that lamp — her faith — is kept alive by divine purpose.

Chapter Eight

Now — About Her Hands

She extends her hand to the poor, yes, she reaches out her hands to the needy.

— Proverbs 31:20

This one woman is representative of so many women. Her theme song is "I'm Every Woman" by Whitney Houston. She's a businesswoman who stretches out her hands to profit and to earn. She has multi-talented hands that hold the keys to her future. Now those same hands are reaching out — not to profit but to show pity, not to collect but to console.

"She extends her hand to the poor." She offers them something, although exactly what we will never know. But we don't need to know. The people she touches know, and that is all that matters.

Even though her life is constantly busy, she never neglects the poor and the needy. She sees people *and* their conditions, which are two entirely different sensitivities.

Our first consideration here is first with the poor; then we are drawn to the needy.

Concerning the poor, a lot of people glance, and many glare. Then there are those who stare with glazed-over eyes, not comprehending the timeless picture before them — the poor, the dirty, the tired, the beggars, the not-so-pretty who have so often out of necessity made the streets their home.

Love Thy Neighbor as Thyself

It is a mental snapshot for all ages — the eyes of the hurting, looking out at a hostile world with a sad expression that wonders, *Why has life been so cruel? Does anyone see me?*

Yes, someone sees you. I admit that many are cold and don't have the heart to be bothered. But many, so many who pass you by simply don't know what to do for you.

This Proverbs 31 lady whom I write about sees you. How do I know? Because she does an incredible thing: She extends her hand, and hands never reach out before the heart does.

Good works, kind deeds, and generous concerns are born deep inside the illumined soul. It's a private place, a place where no one sees — that is, until the heart can keep silent no more. If the heart stays distant, the hands also will be distant.

The woman *sees*; she *feels*; and then, thank God, she *does*!

Like the sun bursting forth its rays, so goodness is an explosion of light. It starts seeping through every dark cloud until every obstacle is cornered, shamed, and then expelled.

When you are kind and good, everyone stands agape. They stare at you, wondering what kind of person you are. But *you* know that you are just a person who sees and does, and for that they are amazed.

This Proverb 31 woman's love is shown not only to her family, but to those she passes every day. They, too, have become a part of her world.

She Sees the Ones the World Forgot

You may ask, "How can I change the world by touching one?" You can't.

"How do I change the world by giving to one who is poor?" You don't.

"On the grand scale, will it really matter what I do?" Well, first of all, whose scale do we use to determine what is grand? Second, the answer is that on earth, it *won't* really matter on a grand scale. But just ask Heaven's opinion, and you'll find the answer is "In Heaven, what you do on earth most definitely *does* matter!"

"If it won't change the world, then what is the purpose?" Simple: to show love, to give joy, to make someone feel for one moment that they matter. And in that moment, a miracle just might occur.

That is a purpose so pure that it bears the mark of the divine. To remind those who seem insignificant in our society that they mean something to somebody is to remind us all that every life has purpose.

We must by our love demonstrate that not all have forgotten, not all ignore, not all just walk by. There are some — indeed, there are many — who see and care, and I purpose to be one of them. Like our "woman of the year" under discussion, I choose to forever extend my hands to the poor and reach out to the needy.

Who are these needy people? Those who lack. Those who are emotionally or physically weak at times. Those who are lonely and sad. Those who need encouragement or seem depressed.

Who are these needy people? Look around; look in the mirror. At one point or another, at some stage of the game, all of us fit in that category. *We* are the needy, and our needs are as diverse as we are.

I used to think that the financially poor were the only ones who were allowed to sing a sad song. I have since learned that those dwelling in makeshift houses have more in common with those dwelling in mansions then either party realizes. We all bleed, we all cry, and we all feel lonely.

My Lord's desire is that I would forever extend my hands to the poor and forever reach out to the needy. You see, I need them as much as they need me. We help each other. We give to each other. The poor and needy have a way of teaching me, of correcting me, of showing me. They reveal a heart of compassion or a heart too busy. They

make me think and feel and keep areas in my heart in check.

In giving, in blessing others, in extending my hands, I am in a way extending *His* hands. Didn't Jesus say concerning the hungry, the thirsty, the stranger, the naked, and those in prison, "Inasmuch as you gave to and took time to love them, you were giving to and loving Me" (Matt. 25:40)?

Maybe that's why we often don't give as we should; we have not seen Jesus in those who are needy. We have not seen Jesus in the eyes of the poor. It may do us well to ask, "How well have I loved You, Lord? How sensitive have I been to Your needs?"

I look differently at the poor and the needy now. I see Jesus in their eyes, longing for me to reach out — and I hope they see Jesus in my eyes. My desire, then, is to forever be a hand extended to help, to comfort, to uplift.

Chapter Nine

Let It Snow, Let It Snow, Let It Snow!

She is not afraid of snow for her household, for all her household is clothed with scarlet.

— Proverbs 31:21

I love to plan. I guess that goes with being a dreamer. Thinking ahead and preparing for the future makes the future a welcomed guest.

Barbies for Future Generations

I remember when I was twelve — many space shuttles ago — something monumental happened: I put away my Barbies.

I loved playing with my Barbies. It was a major part of my childhood. My sister, Stacy, and I played Barbies for

hours each day. At least, that's how I remember it. My mom even built a four-story house for our Barbies to live in.

But it is written:

"There is a time and season for everything" (Eccl. 3:1).
A time to play with toys,
and a time to put those toys away.
But fret not! For every toy tucked neatly away,
a newer, more sophisticated model emerges!

This Barbie house was so cool. It was decorated like a real home. I remember in particular how pretty the bathrooms were. The house even had fireplaces.

My Barbies were a family, and they did family things, such as going to weddings and parties. And, of course, they went to the beach, even though we lived in a suburb of Chicago with no beach in sight. There was even a death in the family, complete with a Barbie-sized funeral.

Do you remember Skipper? She was the kid in the Barbie family. Well, my Skipper had a problem. You see, the more modern Barbie dolls had a wire placed in the legs, along with other gadgets to help them bend and be more flexible. (Before that, all Barbies had stiff, plastic legs.) That wire kept coming out through Skipper's foot. I remember constantly pushing and cramming that wire back up through her foot, but it never stayed put.

Well, what was a girl to do? I assessed the situation and then took action.

Skipper died.

To me, the wire coming out of her foot meant death. Not a painful, slow death — just death. We were not a Christian Barbie family, so I never thought to pray. And why not surgery? I really can't tell you. I just remember that surgery was not an option. Skipper was just dead, plain and simple.

In retelling this story, I realize that it sounds a little like something out of "The Adams Family Values" scrapbook. But I assure you, I did *not* kill Skipper. She died of natural causes — sort of. She gave up the ghost because of that stupid wire!

I used my older sister's wooden jewelry box for the casket. It worked perfectly, and we — all the Barbies and I — had a funeral. I buried that Skipper many years ago, and, most likely, she is still two feet under.

I do recall receiving a new Skipper, and life then returned to normal.

As the years went by — and they do go by — some years hastily hurried along while other years deliberately lingered. But, for the most part, my childhood years took on a life of their own, running at mach speed. And somewhere in between Gumby, Romper Room, Popo Gego, and the Partridge Family, I grew up.

As you grow up, something happens to your eyesight — and I'm not talking about the need for glasses! A sharper and keener focus emerges. The visual senses seem to possess a new, expensive high-powered zoom lens, seeing details missed just a few short years before.

The world looks different. It's still round, but now you perceive angles and perspectives. It's as if you have been

invited to a different side of the planet — a place you knew existed but had never before been allowed entrance. That place was for big people, and that had always been okay with you. As a child, the only country you cared to live in was Toyland, with an occasional trip to "Toys R My Life." What else was living all about?

When my visual senses changed, my outlook changed, and I could never refocus again. I looked at my toys differently now, and I knew what I had to do. All my Barbies were laid to rest, although not exactly as Skipper had been. It's just that the seasons changed. The gale winds of growing up passed by. Time, like the wind, had its way.

I did not give my Barbies away; I put them away. I saved them. I was twelve years old, and I remember saying to myself, *I will save these for my little girl.* I planned way back then for a time not yet seen, but a time I knew would come.

And like a prophet's prediction, that day did come. When my daughter, Brittany, was a little girl, she spent many hours with the very Barbies I played with in my childhood, along with her own Barbie family.

How strange and yet wonderful it was to watch my daughter play with my Barbies. Life appreciates reruns. Brittany is now saving those same Barbies for *her* little girl.

When at age nine my son, Ryan, began feeling the wind of change, he came up to me holding his baseball cleats. Looking up at me with eyes that knew something about life, he said, "Mom, I need some new cleats; these don't fit anymore. I'll save these for my son."

I smiled a strange smile, a sad yet happy smile. I realized it was time to get acclimated once again. The climate of our lives was changing. A new season was nudging its way into our home. My little boy was understanding this thing called growing up; it was now happening to him. And what happens to my children forever affects me.

Get Ready for Each New Season

However, none of us is afraid of new seasons. We're ready.

She is not afraid of snow for her household, for all her household is clothed with scarlet.
— Proverbs 31:21

There is no fear of winter nor of the confining it brings — not when you have planned ahead.

People know winter is coming; its bite is no surprise. Since the beginning of time, time has scripted its dramas. Nature has notified us of her seasons. Winter is an invited guest, and all invited guests are announced.

Rhythmically to the sway of the wind, autumn sings her last song. Each leaf dies a beautiful death, then falls to its grave. Nature's ballet has just performed. A silenced world now sleeps, the seemingly silent world of winter.

What do thoughts of the winter season bring to your mind? My mind plays many movies of winter memories. All scenes, of course, include the bitter coldness, along with that "stay-at-home" and "nowhere-to-go" feeling. At first, that homey feeling can be pleasant. But if it's prolonged, it can lead to "cabin fever."

We sing about the magic of winter, and there is most definitely something awesome and majestic about this strange season. For those protected from winter's temper tantrums, it is a beautiful happening. But if you are left alone to bargain with winter, you surely will not win. If you get too close to winter's wrath, the outcome can be "winter kill."

We must face each life change just as the seasons do. One season bows to the next in humble submission. Each season knows how and when to let go, releasing its hold on an earth that no longer belongs to it. We know nature can be nasty at times, but this time her noble side dresses up and takes a final bow. Nature's segue, if looked at from this angle, is beautiful.

Clothing Ourselves For Life's Storms

Tornado season, hurricane season, rainy season, monsoon season, typhoon season, blizzards, and hailstorms — life can seem like any of these natural storms. The coldness of life with all of its emotional blizzards can chill us to the bone. So what can we do? *We can clothe ourselves.*

We clothe ourselves with garments of praise and peace. We purchase an overcoat of kindness and caring. This is our winter wardrobe, and we spend what we must to get what we need.

And where is faith in this winter attire? It is the fiber woven throughout all we wear. If we *insulate* but don't *isolate* our hearts, we'll stay warm. Staying close to the fire — that's our blanket of hope.

You see, I'm so cozy next to God. Because of Him, I feel more than safe in this unsafe world. He's the Fire that melts the hardened ice. He keeps me from freezing or from becoming too much like the untamed weather.

Life's cruelties are cutting, and the bite of the uncaring can tend to make us like icicles, hard and sharp with a piercing edge. Inner storms can frenzy us as badly as the howling, natural winds we hear and feel. Torrents of tension and monsoon rains of depression seem to threaten our very lives. "Like a tidal wave with unexpected force, so also are problems that blind man's course."

We are often unaware of the turbulent weather that lies hidden behind the seemingly calm exterior of those who stand so near. As for ourselves, waves of worry and winds of doubt mock and dare us to defy their rage. The world wants to drown us — to beat and tear us down so that although we continue to live, we are left in a dazed state, gasping for breath.

Immediate death? Not always. Imminent death? No doubt, through a slow and painful process of killing one dream at a time. Life should play a symphony, but instead we hear a cacophony.

My emotions weary from the struggle; an implosion taunts me. Slow me down, Lord. Help me plan even for the storms. In You, I know that my soul will find a safe haven.

Jesus said that He would never leave us nor forsake us, no matter *what* the weather condition. Blizzards should not take us by surprise either, since there is so much spiritual "weather-tracking equipment" working on our behalf. Like

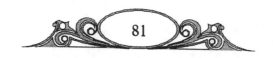

radar, God is working through His Word and through prayer to help us detect the approaching storms.

Better still, we can avoid many of these storms. Like pilots, we must simply stay in constant contact with air-traffic control and refuse to fear the prospect of flying at a higher altitude.

As strange as it may sound, we often are our own weather-making machine, creating the perfect atmospheric conditions for destruction. But with the help of the Holy Spirit, we can see the intensity, path, and potential of these life storms long before they arrive. Thank God, we are not powerless. *Nor do we ever have to be afraid of snow, for all our household is clothed with scarlet.*

So in the bleak and bitter times, stay close to the eternal Fire, and your days will burn with His brightness and His warmth. And remarkably, during what seems to be winter's death grip, spring will hand out an eviction notice.

So it is with faith that does not grow cold. Faith informs fear and discouragement, "You can't stay here any longer."

So we see that it is not only for this virtuous woman's family to be warmed by the fire of faith. It is also by faith that *we* must prepare for any unseen storms ahead. By our faith, the scarcity of winter eventually gives way to spring and summer's abundance. And with that abundance, our family is clothed.

...for all her household is clothed with scarlet.

— **Proverbs 31:21**

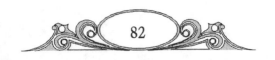

Just Below the Surface

Not too far below the surface of the Mediterranean Sea, hidden within an insignificant shellfish, is found a very special scarlet dye. That's so like God. In His Kingdom, treasures of great value are often found below the surface.

The Hebrew people valued purple or reddish-tinted materials very highly. All of us should desire to clothe our families spiritually with purple — the color that symbolizes what is valued by the Lord.

The question is, how deep are we willing to go below the surface to find the treasures that lie there?

Acutely aware of the dangerous, dimly lighted shafts and tunnels he must travel, a miner looks past where others fear to go, hoping to see that glistening twinkle of gold or other precious jewels. His focus is entirely on the search for a life-changing nugget hidden "just below the surface."

Take the time to look below the surface of *your* life. Look to see how rich you are!

As believers, we have so much gold. In fact, we have found the mother load! Where is this gold I boast of? It's in your family. It's in your children, your husband, your home. It's in your friends; it's in your life. In fact, the treasure you hold *is* your life.

How lavished with treasures we are. Ask yourself, "Are my greatest treasures dressed in royal robes of dignity and confidence? Are they draped with respect and honor?" If so, they, too, are clothed with scarlet.

Chapter Ten

A Little Spare Time? Enjoy It!

She makes tapestry for herself; her clothing is
fine linen and purple.

— Proverbs 31:22

*H*ow about that? The one who never stops is taking a break. I do believe she has a hobby! Verse 22 says, "She makes *for herself.*" Finally! At last, she has a little time to call her own — a few seconds to steal, some laughter to enjoy, a friend to visit, or a book to read over a cup of coffee and a bagel.

It may be just a moment. but it's my moment, and that feels good. I feel young and happy when I have time to dream or play or do whatever I want to do. It's fun to do something for myself once in a while.

And forget any feelings of guilt. No, sir! Not here. When your life is full of work and people and caring for others, a little "me time" is "okay time."

I'm not nurturing nor advocating narcissism. I simply want and desperately need to keep pace with the tempo of life. It passes by too quickly and has a beat all its own.

All musicians understand that in order to be in harmony with the composition, a person must know, feel, and flow with the time signatures. When the timing is off, a work of art designed and created to sound beautiful instead baffles and confuses.

God has made your life a song, so learn how it is to be sung. Stick to the rhythm. Don't try to invent your own.

The Master Musician has perfectly synchronized and measured out the beats according to the eternal orchestration of life. All you need to do is learn His timing. And when you do, watch out! You've just started a chain reaction that leads to something called "walking in the Spirit."

Mirror, Mirror on the Wall — Who in the Heck Am I?

Aren't you and I amazing? We can know so much about duty, obligations, performance, and how to run the lives of our children and our husband. We can even know how to run our communities. Yet we know so little about ourselves! My friend, that isn't a beneficial nor a favorable footing on which to build our lives.

To keep yourself partially sane and to keep from doing the "lulu lunacy dance" under the moonlight one night,

you had better "make for yourself." Your hobby may not be sewing like Miss Nimble Fingers, but do find something to do for just little ol' you.

I'm not talking about self-indulgence here. I'm just talking about self-preservation. I'm talking about *living*, not simply existing.

"She makes tapestries." Well, excuse me! I doubt that I could have survived in the Bible days. Why? Because all women had to sew, not to mention cook and bake. And as far as making tapestries goes — please, give me a break!

A few years back, I assessed my domestic ability and found out I had none. However, like all mothers, I wanted my children to be proud of me.

You know the feeling, we're happy because they are happy that we mommies can make pretty things, or sew pretty things, or cook yummy things — and the list goes on.

Meet My Mentors — My Family

My lack of domestic skills also grated on me because of whom I am related to. I have one of the most impressive, skillful, and creative families one could possibly have. The competition is steep. The lineage begins with a great-, great-, great-, great-grandmother who helped Betsy Ross design and then make no less than the American flag.

In my immediate family, I start with and proudly introduce to you Paul's sister Darlene. (Paul, if you do not know, is the father of my children.) Darlene is the type of person who single-handedly could teach a class entitled "How To

Do Everything." I exaggerate not: She is a walking home economics, art, shop, and dance teacher.

Then there's my sister Steff, who could teach a class entitled "Decorating Until Death." And by her side is Mark, who would teach "How To Build a House While Living in It," and "How To Fix Anything Not Breathing."

Bonnie, the nurse, can perform a colonoscopy and a mammogram on you all at the same time while keeping a home decorated ever so quaint. Steve, my one and only brother, is "Mr. 911." This EMT can miraculously save your life one minute, then meticulously destroy it the next by reading to you from his favorite book, *The Philosophy of Zen.*

And Stacy, my other sister? Well, what can I say? She does everything I just mentioned and more — except instead of boring you with *Zen,* she'll do it with her "blonde" and "dumb men" jokes.

There is so much talent in this one family of mine that I came to the point where I could hardly bear it. So I thought, *I may not be medically-minded, but, by God, I can be creative somewhere!*

Finding That 'Something' I Could Do 'For Myself'

My conversation with myself went something like this. *Okay, let's start with the basics — something non-threatening. Something a neophyte can master. You know, Shoddy, like one of those "Anyone Can Do It" needlework kits, including bantlings.*

I was true to my quest — sort of. You see, I worked on this parrot pattern for four years. The dismal side of the story is that I never finished it.

So then I tried knitting — I seriously did — but all that did was cause piles (no, not *yarn* piles — hemorrhoids!). And I must admit, I *despised* it.

If you don't like knitting but are forcing yourself to do it, it can make you ill and eventually crazy. I know what I'm talking about. I had a creepy encounter in which I almost became a loony tune. Going over the edge became an imminent reality and a little bit too close for comfort.

I vaguely remember that day — the day I broke down. If memory serves me correctly, it happened after four days of sitting, rocking, and knitting.

Four twenty-four-hour days of sitting, rocking, and knitting. Finally, looking comatose, with dilated pupils and mild shock due to constipation, I began to move with an arthritic sort of awkwardness.

With snail-like speed, I cautiously stood up. Snapping, creaking, and cracking, my bones found their place in the world once again. As the physical activity of standing took its toll, I knew I was flirting with death or a possible stroke. Finally, the feat was accomplished, and all the anxiety that had been pent up for four days exploded.

I became like one drugged and delirious. I ran full force straight through the screen door into the neighborhood, screaming wildly!

As I ran, I dragged behind me a one-mile-long, eight-inch-wide *knitted* burial shroud. The ripped-off screen from

the door outlined my sickly body and pressed firmly against my deranged-looking face. Tightly gripped in both my hands were those psycho-looking knitting needles. (For some reason, in my therapy sessions, we had not gained enough ground to get me to release those things from my grip. However, we *were* able to ascertain that knitting was not for me!)

Imagine if I lived way back in Bible times! I can see it now: *The Jerusalem Journal* headline would read, "Woman Died of Strangulation While Making Tapestry." The article would say, "All who watched the incident thought it was a joke until it was too late. If we can untangle her from the weaving loom, funeral services will be tomorrow."

Get a Life!

I've heard it said, *"Get a life!"* Well, that's what I was trying to do. But one thing I figured out all on my own: I wasn't going to find it in needlework, knitting, or sewing!

Sewing is not my thing, but it may be yours. And if not sewing, there has to be *some* fun thing that you like to do. Maybe it's reading a book, working in the garden, decorating, sky diving, or mud wrestling. I don't know what it is, but I know there is something enjoyable out there for you.

Is there anything that calls your name? For me, it's writing, decorating, and singing. I love to sing, but at one time, I wasn't quite sure singing loved *me.* So I made some time for myself to take voice lessons.

In all of us, there is a talent to perfect, a life to enjoy, a story to write or to tell or to sing. In you and in me, there is a God-given gift.

Take time to find out what yours is. Stop wasting your years wondering, *Who in the heck am I*? Look inside and find out! Make a difference; dream some dreams; set some goals. And as you pursue your dream, your eyes will once again be like those of a child, full of wonder and a sense of adventure.

Do be a little realistic, though. For instance, if you weigh three hundred pounds and you like it that way, your dream of becoming a supermodel might be somewhat unattainable. But then again, "Big Momma" model agencies are pulling their weight these days, so go for it!

And remember — schedule a day every couple of weeks or at least a few hours in each day that belong to you. If you don't take some time for yourself, life begins to lose meaning. Follow the example of the virtuous woman, who *"...makes tapestry FOR HERSELF."*

Proverb 31:22 also says, *"...her clothing is fine linen and purple."* That means Mom is adorned with the very garments her family wears — and even better! She is not in rags, curlers, and cold cream (thank the Almighty!). She is neither worn out nor resentful of her responsibilities in the home. She is clothed with fine linen and purple.

Much more than that, she is clothed with a purpose and a passion for living. Of all her clothing, that outfit is the nicest.

She wears life so well. How does she do it? Well, for one thing, she knows all about Chapter Six. Remember? *She girds herself with strength.* She is also disciplined and organized, and she takes care of herself. I bet she even likes herself.

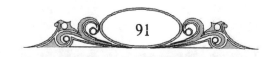

Do you like yourself? I sure hope so. It is much easier to like those around you when you like *yourself.*

You see, we often project upon others and judge others according to how we feel about ourselves, our personal life, and the circumstances that surround us.

A Word From One Who Enjoys Life

If every minute belongs to everybody else, you are losing a portion of *your* existence. God gave you a life — a life wherein you can learn and grow and become. What a great thought: *to become something.* To work and dream and pray. To be in the process of realizing great potential.

Becoming. Challenged to change! It's limitless. It is as vast as the universe. This *becoming* process keeps us young and full of purpose. I am both scared, excited, and sobered by the sheer amazement of it all.

So make a life that reflects *you.* Don't become a shadow. A shadow has no substance.

And a quick word to the unmarried: Find a man or woman who understands how important you are and how important it is to be in the blooming stages of *becoming.* Settle for nothing less.

Chapter Eleven

While He Sits

Her husband is known in the gates, when he sits among the elders of the land.

She makes linen garments and sells them, and supplies sashes for the merchants.

— Proverbs 31:23,24

*V*erse 23 really irritates me. This woman cooks, sews, shops, sells, weaves, owns companies, and has outreach ministry to the poor. She plants and plows her own vineyard and willingly works with her hands. (At this point, I would be ready for a padded cell!) And what does the husband do?

He sits!

Oh, brother! I can't stand it. He sits with other men talking about only God knows what. They probably are debating about which wife is most worn out. Of course he's

known in the gates — the entire city gossips about how lazy he is!

Here's a side note: Have you ever noticed while watching news reports from poor, developing countries who are the ones working? *Women,* that's who! Who do you see carrying the water pots on their heads, pounding the husks off the rice, working as vendors, or squatting near some fire cooking or by the river beating dirt out of soiled clothing? *Women.*

And what does a woman have to look forward to in some of those countries? In India they are still debating about "bride-burning" if the in-laws don't like the dowry. And where is the man? He helps light his wife on fire; then he goes out to fulfill some religious duty that will produce absolutely nothing for his family or his people!

Religious men who are angry and blinded are often cruel to their women. It seems to be a mockery. But in reality, it is an open demonstration and pronouncement to the falseness of the religion.

Gee, some side note — I'm depressed!

Thank God, women according to the Bible are to be loved and honored! Thank God, the Hebrew woman of ancient days were respected and cherished.

The Virtues of Sally Seamstress

Now, where were we? Oh, yes, we're back to Sally Seamstress. She is too busy to concern herself with the daily sitting habits of the elders of the city. If they want to talk the day away, that's fine with her. She has garments to

make and linens to sell. She's not sad or sidetracked. She's got stuff to do.

Personally, I would wear sackcloth to mourn my too-busy life, feeling as if I was carrying a little too much of the load. But no sackcloth for her. No death in her attitude — just life, *lots* of life.

> **Her husband is known in the gates, when he sits among the elders of the land.**
> **She makes linen garments and sells them, and supplies sashes for the merchants.**
> **— Proverbs 31:23,24**

As her husband is known, so is she. She sees the need and gets to work. What great business sense this woman of excellence possesses! She is the mentor for all womankind. I'd like to have her visit some of those countries where women do most of the work. She could teach the men who live there a thing or two!

You can bet your last shekel that those men who sit around and talk in the city where this woman lives will all be wearing new sashes tomorrow. Although they are elders, they are also merchants. Soon they'll be walking around advertising her "Sashes Galore" shop that just opened!

A Great Man in This Story

Get some coffee or tea, or better yet, a double expresso. You will need it for this one!

Let's backtrack a moment: There is a husband we need to chit chat about. Earlier I joked about him sitting around all day long, because some men actually do that. But not this man in Proverbs 31.

What I want you to notice is this: Look at the kind of woman this husband has made. I say he has *made* her with all due respect to women everywhere. It's a fact; husbands help create the wife they live with, just as wives help create the husband they live with. We're all not as independent as we think we are.

You and I are made in the image of God. And because of that, we all have a God-given ability and responsibility to *create.* But that is just the beginning. After creating, we are to take care of what we have given life to.

People create people, and the cycle never ceases. But we create more than our children. We create our families' disposition. Our priorities become their priorities. Thus, to a large degree we create our children's values — at least for a while anyway.

We not only create our children biologically, (and we don't really "create" them; we simply "house" them), we create them emotionally and psychologically. We actually form and mold a person.

We have the power to subdue the world we live in. How potent this force is that has been given to us! Unlike animals who live by *instinct,* you and I live by *choices.* We all have within us the power to tear down or to build up, to hurt or to help, to contour a life or to crush it — especially within our family.

Men, more than women, seem to exercise their inherent ability to create a world or to destroy it. They have such strength. They have such power. And they often use this power to create, or to influence, the woman they choose as their wife.

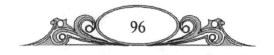

Any confident lady who is reading this may be cringing at this point. But let's face it — the world is full of women who need a man to set the course for their lives. In and of itself, that is not wrong.

As women, we are the weaker vessel (1 Peter 3:7), and, like it or not, all vessels have support beams. It's not weakness to need another's strength; we were made that way. We need a man to love us, to want us, to be tender to us, and to support us. We need their strength; we rely on that power.

Be careful, though. If left unchecked, that need becomes feeble and frail. Then *we* become feeble and frail.

That is why woman take so much abuse and put up with extreme offenses that a man would never put up with. Men are so strong and self-consumed, and often we women rely on that strength far too much — until one day a tragedy happens. We stumble about, not realizing that we have misplaced our own strength and free will — our own personhood.

When that happens in our marriage, we begin to lose confidence, purpose, and personal zeal with each weakened day. And the most personal of all zeal that stands in jeopardy is our *spirit.* Spirit — the source of the very purpose and passion that keeps this story alive — is the zeal that the woman I write about has harnessed so well.

How sad that, if the men we love and need so much begin to hurt us, we seem to need them even more. You see, weakness and frail emotions attract abuse. The fact is, we do need our men, but not in a way that cripples.

In the course of life, we women often lose sight of who we really are. So when and if the time comes for us to stand alone, we cannot. We find there is no one to fight for us any longer. But the truth is, the main reason we may one day find ourselves having to fight alone is that long ago we abandoned ourselves, little by little.

Hopefully, through this book, your Bible, and other good books as well, you are getting reacquainted with yourself. Don't be too shocked by what you uncover.

The fact is, we women are loaded with power! The authority and competence we walk in is jarring to me. Men know we have this hormonal birthright of influence, and it scares them.

Come on, think about it. Who is responsible for Proverbs 31 in the first place? Lemuel's mom. She is using her God-given right to coach her son concerning what kind of woman he should look for and eventually marry. But even before that, she is instructing her son, the king, on how to maintain his kingship.

Deep down inside, men are afraid of women! Why else do you think men all over the world feel that they have to dominate women? With one certain kind of a look, a woman can weaken a man, tempt a man, or torment a man. Another look can strengthen, encourage, and vindicate. (No doubt, of course, you and I choose the *latter* looks!)

The fact that we women have a superior command of our language and our vocabulary causes the most educated of men to be silenced. We are a wise and wonderful invention. The Bible even says of us wives that we are a good thing (Prov. 18:22).

Proverbs 31 is not about what a woman must do. It is about who she *is* — creative, resourceful, and multi-talented; a lover, a friend, a minister, and a mother. She is perceptive in the full spectrum of life.

But if this lady is great — and she is — we need to admire her man! What a guy he is. This man is incredible. Secure and confident, he doesn't have to put her down to feel accomplished. He knows who he is and who he is not. Now, that's a lesson to be learned!

He also knows who his wife is not. Observe this man carefully, please; look at what he has done. He has "allowed" his wife freedom and expression and a life. He is letting her live and, thus, being rewarded for it.

He knows well the story of the Garden, when God breathed into man, and man became a living soul. The woman was present, too, all snug and safe within that first man. Her life was hidden inside the man, and this man understands that.

And the woman's life is still all wrapped up in the man's. This husband knows what he can do *to* her; instead, he lives by what he can do *for* her. For he knows the part of the story where the first man was alone and longing. Man is empty without the woman, for she used to be inside of him. So this husband shyly admits to himself that he is dependent on his wife and needs her terribly.

He is not the anchor to her dreams. He isn't jealous of her either; he is *proud* of her. I'm sure she amazes him by all she does, and quietly he is proud of himself. He sees other frustrated women who want to be free to dream and enjoy life as his wife does.

Of course "he is *known* in the gates"! And of course the city talks about him. He's a "one-of-a-kind" type of man! Some of the talk is rough. Weak men put him down, saying he doesn't control his wife. Others say she rules the roost. This husband admits that all women rule the roost, but his woman does not rule *him*.

But most of the talk speaks of this husband's love for his wife. Most of the talk enhances his right to "sit among the elders of the land."

Maybe that's why he is known; certainly we are all known by the group we hang out with. He has taken time to sit with those greater than himself, and what he has learned he has applied; it is seen in his woman. Her fervor for life is flamed by his favor toward her.

Chapter Twelve

Man, She Looks Good!

Strength and honor are her clothing; she shall rejoice in time to come.

— Proverbs 31:25

This "woman of the hour" whom we're discussing knows something about how to shop and how to dress. She knows how to make herself pretty. She can identify with women from the beginning of time who have embarked on that eternal quest to look pretty.

We "modern Proverbs 31 women" are no different; we're on that same quest. For instance, when most of us go shopping for clothes, we select attire according to our body structures.

I personally cannot wear anything that has vertical lines unless I want to look like a light pole. I am six feet tall and

thin. (I used to be thinner, but, anyway, I am still tall!) If I try to wear a vertically striped jacket, I look ten feet tall. So the *way* I wear clothes determines the clothes I wear.

Have you ever seen (I know you have) an overweight person wearing stretch knit pants with a halter top? Scary, huh? If you wanted to (but of course, you don't), you could count the cellulite indentations. But none of us would be that rude, would we?

I'm not trying to be judgmental, because, as thin as I am, my back end has its own set of problems. So what's my point? If we want to be the least bit fashionable, and if we want to find any measure of success on our quest to look our best, all of us should shop according to what we can wear well on our own body shapes.

There's Nothing Wrong With Wanting To Be Beautiful

Much of a lady's time is spent trying to look pretty. And we should look pretty because most of humanity — especially men, and certainly husbands everywhere (unless they're slobs) — more than appreciates the effort.

Before I began studying the clothing, cosmetics, and customs of the Old Testament Hebrew women, I always conjured up images of tired, very dull, and dowdy ladies in my mind.

Oh, boy, was I *wrong*! Were the women in the Old Testament unappealing? Not in the least. On the contrary, they could really *dress*! Even the men liked to look sharp.

For the trendy man in fashion of Bible times, there was general wear that included the following: inner garment, girdle, outer garment, purse, and sandals. For those special occasions, the fashion statement would include several extra items: robes of honor, wedding garments, mourning garments, winter garments, ornaments, rings, and amulets. For dessert, the fashion menu topped off the ensemble with an appropriate hairstyle and headdress. This made up the fashionable Hebrew man of the Old Testament.

For ladies, their wardrobe back then would include the following: inner garment, outer garment (hey, where's the girdle?), veil, handkerchief, sandals, ornaments, bracelets, anklets, earrings, nose jewels (don't let my daughter see that item!), crisping pins, cosmetics, and perfumes. Hair styling would include braids and headdress.[13]

That list hits close to home, doesn't it? Are we talking here about the past, the present, or what?

A Woman's Beauty Throughout the Ages

The bottom line is that throughout the ages, woman's beauty has somehow always come forth. Never mind the century these Old Testament women found themselves in. Women are women, and they are beautiful throughout and for all time.

One thing is for sure: A woman knows how to be lovely, and she *wants* to be lovely. That is without a doubt a part of being a *woman*.

I can envision these ancient "an-sisters" of mine getting ready for the day or for a party, a funeral, or a wedding. At a wedding, I see the young people giggle and talk about what the bride and groom will be doing "after the reception." I see the teenagers putting on that adolescent air of "Here I come!"

I see the older, still unmarried people watching the festivities, a little sad that this day does not belong to them. I see a mother holding her daughter's hand one last time, wiping away timeless tears that say, "My baby has grown up, and now she's leaving me."

Reflecting on what it was like back in ancient days isn't hard to do because it is so much like my own life today. Living back then was much like life is now in many of the heart and soul issues of life.

Then as now, there was the art of living and loving, dealing with problems, raising children, hating war, watching life begin, and watching it end. In every culture, through every age, man's common experience has been life and death and all the events caught in between.

Life throughout the ages sings a similar song. The chorus sounds the same. The beat and the bridge might be different, but the lyrics are familiar to all of us.

The Garments of Strength and Honor

We've talked about a woman's concern about fabrics, inner and outer garments, and so on. But now we are told of another garment that should be part of a woman's daily

attire: *strength and honor.* The Bible says that strength and honor are this virtuous woman's clothing (Prov. 31:25).

How do we add strength and honor to our wardrobes? These qualities are acquired as almost everything is in life: little by little.

This lady whom we're studying studies fashion. A major percentage of her life centers around what people wear. From dawn to dusk, it's retail; it's materials; it's sashes; it's sewing and weaving and sewing some more. She sees the emphasis placed on what we adorn ourselves in. It is her business to see. She is an expert about what is stylish and what is affordable.

Yet she also understands that we are ultimately found disrobed if all that we cover ourselves with is visible clothing. Strength and honor must also be worn, with as much elegance as the loveliest, most expensive dress.

Clothing is tagged and priced, but *strength* and *honor* are monetarily priceless. However, to wear these two priceless qualities will cost you your life.

It takes years to weave these garments called strength and honor. The threads are woven together by tears, adversity, and trial. Does that surprise you? How else do you think strength and honor are earned? The truth is, before you put on the finished garments, your every conviction will be tested, your every secret motive challenged.

To *wear* these garments is to *be* them. To possess this royal heavenly garb, a part of you must die. You have to die to your own will and "want to." You die to the little god reflected in the mirror who will go to any length to save and satisfy himself.

You see, a prideful person cannot wear honor because somewhere in life, humility paved honor's way (that's *paved*, not *paid*!).

And what about strength? Where does it come from? What is it really? If we understand true strength, maybe then we can capture it.

I know strength when I see it, and I feel afraid when strength is not present. I know its intensity. Like the air I breath and the wind around me, I cannot grasp it. But without it, I cannot live.

So much like God is this thing called strength. It's far too majestic for man in himself to wear. So what does God do? He dresses us. He covers us with His very own garments.

Now I see; it is my Father's cloak. Strength is *His* covering. It is beautiful. It is the color of water, transparent and pure. Unlike water, however, it cannot be penetrated. Nor can it be daunted or dented.

All who wear this garment of His strength walk openly and unashamed. They live visible to the world, regardless of what is revealed.

Strength is the most humble of all attire, whereas honor is a covering quilted in confidence. Strength is worn by all who walk close to God. It is given to help love Him, to serve Him, and to be like Him.

They can try to strip me of my dignity, mar my destiny, and mock my mission. But I will never be found naked. I am and always will be dressed in a distinguished manner, for strength and honor are my clothing.

An honorable man will serve in silence and in obscurity with the same spirit of excellence he would if the crowds were watching. A person of genuine strength and honor knows that *God* is watching; no other eyes matter.

At times you may serve Him publicly where applause can be heard, where approval pats you on the back, where the sound of appreciation is sweet. But be careful! Whether or not you receive man's praise simply should not matter.

It should not matter *where* we serve, only that we do serve, whether it is on a crude or fancy stage, in the workplace or at home. An honorable person knows that he does not need man's recognition to be recognized.

God sees all. Therefore, I am concerned only with this: "That in Him I live and move and have my being." *Therein strength and honor stands.*

Chapter Thirteen

Ready or Not, Here I Come!

...she shall rejoice in time to come.

— Proverbs 31:25

*T*he future is looking GOOD! Although I haven't seen it yet, it's pretty clear. That's the Proverbs 31 woman's approach to life!

When strength and honor are our clothing, we, too, shall rejoice in the days to come. There's nothing to fear; we're dressed and ready to go. Go where? To meet the future, of course. It's been waiting on us. It plays a timeless game.

So ready or not, here I come!

Knowing that the future is coming torments a lot of people. But it doesn't torment me. You see, I play that timeless game too. I say to the relentless calendar, "Ready or

not, here I come!" I truly rejoice, knowing that the once far-off day is drawing near.

Apprehension doesn't stymie me; anticipation *stirs* me. I allow no foreboding to hover over my days. They are *my* days! God and I own them. I will not permit any seen or unseen force to cloud my life. I will not allow the future to depress me or give me a heart attack, high blood pressure, or hives!

You see, it's really a matter of faith. If faith sees the unseen God and believes in His unseen hand at work in this earth, then why fear?

I hate the question, "Why fear?" because the only answer to that question is that we are so human. It is the hallmark of fallen humanity to fear and to doubt. Sin has branded us. At times, *all* of us fail to focus in on God. Even those of us who call ourselves believers have been doubters far too often.

This is our earth struggle. Our "good fight" is the fight of faith, which refers to fighting to keep faith alive, *not* fighting others because of our faith! We battle in prayer against the foes that try to strip our faith of its privileges, arresting in the name of the Lord that which would paralyze our right to rule and reign in life.

Faith in God Takes Care of Every Need

When you walk with the Lord and wear His garments of strength and honor, you will not be found naked in the days of scarcity.

Faith in God will feed you in the day of famine. It focuses on God's Word and on God's promises, not on the world's empty and deluded "maybes." Faith may quiver a bit, but never does it crumble.

A person of faith stands. He may be bowed over a little by adversity, but, nonetheless, he rises in the middle of lack and sings because his heart dwells in the day of plenty.

I live in God's provisions. Some are tangible; some are untouchable at this present time. Nevertheless, all are mine.

Rejoice in the Time To Come

Do not lose heart! Look up and see! The sky is big, and bigger still is our God.

When you lose heart, it's as if a rainy, gloomy day has just been poured on your emotions — the kind of day where the sun has a temper tantrum, stomping its feet and refusing to shine. Losing heart is the saddest of all emotions. It is the bruise no one sees. It is the death of you that no one notices.

Silent souls, those who have lost heart in their future, walk among us weeping, unheard.

> **Unless the Lord had been my help, my soul would soon have settled in silence.**
>
> **— Psalm 94:17**

Here's a poem I wrote for all the sad and silent souls. May you resound with life once again and "rejoice in the time to come"!

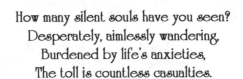

How many silent souls have you seen?
Desperately, aimlessly wandering,
Burdened by life's anxieties,
The toll is countless casualties.

Wounded people bruised in heart,
The zeal of the spirit seems to depart.
Like a tidal wave with unexpected force —
So are problems, they blind our course.

BE SILENT NO MORE...
For there is a Light who gives hope to all men,
And life to the spirit to be born again.

But what about us who have walked with Him?
We know His name; we're redeemed from sin,
When a cloak of sorrow and depression comes,
Clouding the life-giving rays of the Son?

WHAT DO I DO WHEN LONELINESS HAS BECOME
A TAUNTING FRIEND?
This is what I do —
I linger long with Him.
And then (there will always be a then),
The soul starts to laugh,
For the silent season begins to pass.

"She shall rejoice in the time to come" —
and so shall we!

Regardless — Relish the Moments!

So make it your aim to relish every moment of every day. Life is good if you choose to look at life as good.

Concerning our Proverbs 31 woman, we don't read of her heartaches and days of depression. But I know for certain that she has them. How do I know? Because she is alive. And life on earth as we know it is facing one conflict after another.

How else do I know that she has her own set of frustrations? For starters, she is like you and me — human. She is not from another planet, although she may wish that she were at times. Gravity keeps her feet on the ground, just as it does ours.

And with that great revelation, we realize that this woman had the same opportunities to give up and quit as we all do. Furthermore, she works (self-employed), so we know that she deals with rude and irritating people. She also has a husband sitting around somewhere, so we know she deals with being misunderstood and ignored at times.

This Proverbs 31 woman has children, so we know her life is hectic, hurried, and, on more occasions than she wants to count, sleepless. Dear me! How human do we want her to be? There's enough potential frustration here to last an entire life span!

She lives in a community; therefore, she feels its troubles. She sees power, prejudice, and injustice at play among those in authority and tries to understand the local politics and scandals. She deals with family problems as well. In her house full of kids, an argument most certainly erupts every

so often. She deals with merchants and customers on a daily basis. She lives this experience called life.

This woman has been talked about. She has been wrongly accused. She has cried herself to sleep when no one noticed. She has felt the betrayal of a friend. She has also most likely been undermined in business, unless people back then were more scrupulous then they are now. For some reason, I doubt it.

These difficult experiences were the "school" where so many of this virtuous woman's life lessons were learned. That's where strength and honor became her clothing.

And regardless of what she has gone through, she still laughs and loves. That's what I like about her — she has that "regardless" kind of attitude. "Regardless of what the world dishes out, I am still accountable to be the best human being I can be."

That makes all the difference in the world — *being accountable.*

What else makes this woman so special? It's the clothes she wears, the God she serves, the way she handles the minutes and hours she is given. It is her faith! She understands faith's eternal framework in this temporal world. No matter what has happened, her future is looking good!

Chapter Fourteen

Say, 'Aaah' —
A Word About Opening
Our Mouths

She opens her mouth with wisdom, and on her tongue is the law of kindness.

— Proverbs 31:26

*Y*our feet hang lifeless, dangling from a crisp, vinyl, paper-lined examining table. You're wearing nothing but panties and a paper robe that you will get to take home after your visit — a nice robe you can cut up into nice squares to use for paper towels, if you so desire.

You are nervous and frostbitten due to the Arctic climate you have been sitting in — half-naked, mind you — for the past two hours. The doctor walks in.

"Hello," he says. You wonder why he is so darn cheery. Then you realize the reason: The doctor realizes that he is healthy, and you are not. And for his added benefit, you now have bronchial pneumonia as a result of his frigid office and will need his additional services for the next six months.

You are certain, due to the icicles that have formed on the windows, that he will reach for the doctor's best friend, "the pharmacopoeia," to find out how to deal with a frozen patient. Instead, he reaches for a tongue depressor — the doctor's *other* best friend. (Well, anyway, you were close!)

You know what's coming next. (I gag just thinking about it!) It is time for the checkup to begin. Step one is for the doctor to cram a smooth, splinter-free (you hope) piece of bark down your soon-to-be-sore throat. You felt fine before that intrusive act, but now you are a real, bona fide sick person.

The gag reflex is different in all of us. My sister, for example, gags while brushing her teeth. On the other hand, when a doctor has to look into my stomach by way of my mouth and esophagus, I usually don't gag. I just get goggle-eyed, and my body becomes stiff.

I have always questioned why a doctor wants to look down your throat when you go to him because your back hurts. What is it he wants to see in there? But without a word of opposition, you obey as he says, "Open up and say 'Aaah!'"

All through life, someone is telling us to open our mouths. As babies, a spoon loaded with slop becomes an "airplane" ready to land in the "hanger." Mommy says,

"Here it comes — open wide!" And from that moment on, gagging is a part of life.

Here We Go Again

I'm sitting on cold vinyl once again. This time I am reclining and fully dressed. The surroundings look like a torture chamber, twenty-first-century style. The room reeks of formaldehyde and other alien odors.

The dentist enters, whose face I have never seen completely. I am familiar only with his beady eyes, even though I have been his patient for the last ten years. It appears he is carrying a gaff. Looking like a robber and somewhat crazed, he demands that I open my mouth.

"Wider. Wider, please... *wider!*" Does he want to check my teeth or my intestines?

It's just one more setting where we are requested to "Open thy mouth."

Years ago I took voice lessons, and, sure enough, I heard the same command from my voice teacher: "Open wide." I was in class one day, doing vocalization. I already felt stupid because I knew how I looked, not to mention how I sounded. "Now," the teacher said, "sit up straight, open your mouth, and sing."

"M-e-e-e-e-e-e-o," I sang.

"Again."

"M-e-e-e-e-e-e-o," I sang again.

"Mrs. Chase, please open your mouth wider."

Okay, you asked for it, I thought. Then I belted out the best *"M-E-E-E-E-E-E-O"* I had!

"Mrs. Chase, not that wide," she scolded me.

So there we have it. The balancing act continues between how much of our mouth to open and how much of it to keep shut. I've been working on that one all my life!

'She Opens Her Mouth With Wisdom'

Oh, boy! There's a task for the human race. Can you imagine that every time you verbally confronted a situation or spoke out an opinion, it would be a word from the wise?

Dear Wisdom, lend me your ear. May I speak to you for a moment? Can we ever hear about you too much? Can we ever have too much of you?

Wisdom simply responds, "No."

The search to find and to become saturated with wisdom is without end. If Jesus could and did increase in wisdom, why would I ever park my desire for wisdom in neutral? I must keep learning. We all must continue to press on and into this invaluable treasure.

The gaining of wisdom is painful. And like all things spiritual, the first mountain to be removed to obtain it is *pride.*

When we do not learn from wisdom's gentle hand, life takes over. Lessons not learned before are now taught harshly, and the new teacher can be so cruel.

She opens her mouth with wisdom, and on her tongue is the law of kindness."

— Proverbs 31:26

Wisdom is a friend of waiting, and in waiting there is silence — at times, awkward silence. Yet in this silence, great things are heard and understood. Wisdom soars above the situations and sees many outcomes. Good decisions are then made because of what wisdom sees. Neither anger nor pride can see what wisdom sees — they are both blind and kingdoms apart from where wisdom resides.

Who Is This Woman?

We have not been talking about a silent, shy saint. This woman is scary. Thank God, she is on our side! We have here a woman who knows not only *how* to speak, but *when* to speak. That combination creates empires.

This is potential greatness right before our eyes. What she speaks and how she speaks makes her what she is.

"...And on her tongue is the law of kindness." Do you realize that this lady understands a mystery? She has unlocked one of the fabulous laws that govern life. The unraveling of all hidden things rests on laws, whether natural or spiritual, for the Kingdom of Heaven is governed by God's law. And this woman operates according to one of those heavenly laws — the law of kindness.

The working of all wonders — every miracle, every answered prayer — is a discovery of one of God's laws. That is why we seek Him and His Kingdom, so we can fully understand.

That's why Jesus gave us several "the Kingdom of Heaven is like unto" parables. Those parables unwrap heavenly mysteries right before our eyes. A door opens up in our spirit; then light shines in and shows us secrets about the workings of God. These discoveries are what makes our spiritual journey worth the while.

Let us start with the *law of kindness* upon our tongues and see where it takes us.

Words Reveal What We Seek To Conceal

I invite you, my friend, to sit down and speak with me. You will reveal your heart and I mine. We can hide but for a moment from one another. Our opinions, our likes and dislikes, and our attitudes — they are all expressed in *words.* Words used to conceal actually reveal.

By words and deeds, the invisible spirit of each of us — our characters, our dispositions — is now seen! So soon you let me know you. I hear not only what you say, but what you do not say. Topics you *don't* speak about show me many things about you that you thought were veiled.

We communicate unceasingly in various ways. May it be the way of wisdom that we reveal. For there is no way around it and no mystery to it — in one way or another, we *will* reveal ourselves.

Your heart is revealed by the words you speak. Therefore, words are like a compass for your character. That's why it's important to check your words every now

and then, just to make sure you're going in the right direction.

Words of wisdom, if heeded, can save our lives. This woman's wisdom is not shrouded; it is shared, for it says, "She opens her mouth." This insightful person knows how much her words are needed.

Like you, I have seen my words lift a person from despair. I have also seen my words bruise and cause a countenance to fall. I have seen the power of my words. It awakens me! It startles me to realize my words have the power to speak and affect a life!

We should well remember that when we speak, God is one of the listeners. How often we forget.

We are artists, you know, adding color and contrast, depth and perception to life's backdrop. Our tongue is like the artist's brush.

Speaking the Truth in Love

Sometimes the greater love is not speaking, but listening.

Maybe you can relate to this: You are a person who likes to have detailed conversations in which you have the opportunity to express how you feel. (Some may call that being opinionated; I call it being interesting.) You enjoy talking about what is happening in the world and what should not be happening in the world according to your way of thinking.

Well, if that is you, you have just met another one like you — me! So what does that mean? It can mean many

things, it can mean many hard times are ahead, such as having to wait instead of pounce, slow down instead of rush in. It means holding on for a while to that "truth" you so desperately have to "share," no matter how painful it is to do that.

I have been around not only individuals who have no control over their tongue, but ministers who believe it is their duty and divine call to correct everyone in their path. I used to think I was outspoken until I came in contact with a few self-appointed "prophets of tongue-lashing." Using as their justification the words, "Open rebuke is better than hidden love" (Prov. 27:5), they dominate people and entire congregations by holding over their heads the unspoken threat of being shamed and publicly humiliated.

I believe part of glorifying my Heavenly Father includes guarding the words my mouth speaks. In both my private and public life, my desire is that I would "let my light so shine among men, that they might see my good works and glorify my Father in Heaven" (Matt. 5:16).

I have learned, and by His grace I continue to learn, that there is a greater strength than *saying* what you *feel*, and that is *feeling* what you are about to *say*. At times truth can be cold and crushing. Wisdom feels and is tender.

"*...And on her tongue is the law of kindness.*" Wisdom waits and is patient. If it is not kindly spoken, it is not in the family of wisdom. The things you say can be direct, but the words must be spoken tenderly.

Speak Now or Forever Hold Your Peace?
(Or Was That 'Hold Your *Piece*'?)

"But I don't want to hold my piece (a piece of my mind, that is). They need what I am about to say."

Well, then, go ahead, Big Mouth! Give them all a piece of your mind! But be assured — you will not have any *peace* in your mind!

Although I like debating — better said, discussing the delicate issues of our day — I am not a hothead, spouting off about every little matter. I've learned, and I am still learning, how to let some things go. I've had to learn. I have found a greater discipline in being quiet — or, more accurately, in knowing when to speak, for quiet I will never be.

Until the trumpet is sounded, I think it shall be my life's toil to endeavor to tame this tongue. And such a wrestling match it is at times.

Do me a favor — just for one day, listen to the way you talk. Hear with humble ears what comes out of your mouth. After all, everyone else has to. You may be shamed, shocked, or pleasantly surprised.

A Simple Test Could Save the Day

Have you ever heard of an aptitude test? I'm sure you have. That type of test is great. All you do is answer a few questions, and bingo! You know with a good measure of probability your calling and vocation in life.

Taking an aptitude test reveals your strengths and weaknesses. After completing the test, you never again have to wander around wondering what it is you are supposed to do with the rest of your life.

Another Kind of Test: The 'I.P.C.B.A.B.M.'

This entire book was born out of one desire — to help you in every area of your life. Therefore, all of us here at S.U.L.M. (*"shut up and listen ministries"*) have designed another kind of test. This test will pinpoint and verify if you might be suffering from being (excuse me for saying) a blabbermouth.

You can take this test in a counselor's office, a psychologist's office, or the mental ward. But in order to protect your reputation, dear reader, I have made it possible for you to take this confidential test in the privacy of your own humble abode.

This I.P.C.B.A.B.M. test (the "I Possibly Could Be a Blabbermouth" test) goes by classified and secret names so that if you choose to order this test by mail, no one will suspect the contents of the package.

For example, this confidential package might have one of the following coded names on the return address:

- T.B.M.P.T. (The "Blabbermouth Privacy Test")
- M.M.I.A.R.G.A. ("My Mouth Is a Rudder Gone Amok" test)
- M.T.J.E. ("My Tongue Just Exploded" test)
- M.W.A.L.V. ("My Words Are Like Vomit" test)

- T.T.I.M.M.I.R.M.L. ("That Thing in My Mouth Is Ruining My Life" test)

Here are a few sample questions from page 1:

- How do you start a sentence?
- How do you end a conversation?
- What kind of feeling do you leave with those you have conversed with?
- Do you add life and joy and exuberance when you speak?
- Do you bring grace to the hearers of your words?

See, that wasn't so bad, was it? Now let's continue — take a deep breath, exhale, and relax.

Here are a few sample questions from page 2:

- When people see you approaching, do they violently scream and begin to run away?
- While you are speaking, are two or more people throwing up?
- Has Satan ever appeared while you were in the middle of "correcting" someone, nodding and smiling his approval? Did you dismiss the fact that Satan occasionally appears while you are talking as coincidence?
- Has anyone ever paid you to shut up?
- Have you ever thought it strange that all your closest friends are deaf even though you have never used sign language a day in your life?
- Have you recently found out that your children tell their friends they are orphans and you are a distant relative so they won't be embarrassed by what you say?

- Have you ever received hate mail with graphic pictures of someone yanking your tongue out of your mouth?
- Have you noticed that you are only invited to parties after you have been diagnosed with acute laryngitis?

Well, ol' Buddy, ol' Pal, you can get up now. Groveling and begging for forgiveness will do you no good. There's just one answer: Adjust the rudder, friend. The ship has been longing to take you in a new direction for a long, long time.

Numbing Your Own Heart

You see, when we talk with a negative edge, we lose insight and the ability to discern rightly. Eventually we numb our hearts and actually become negative people. When that happens, foolish mistakes become comfortable and at home with us.

How different things would be if you and I would make sure we don't hush wisdom's whisper! But so often we do silence that quiet nudge. And when we do, we allow the loudness of life to be heard and felt, drowning out the Counselor within who is sent to help guard our words and guide our way.

She opens her mouth with wisdom, and on her tongue is the law of kindness.

— Proverbs 31:26

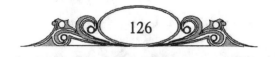

Chapter Fifteen

The All-Seeing Eye

*She watches over the ways of her household,
and does not eat the bread of idleness.*

— Proverbs 31:27

*H*ave you ever seen a picture of that huge pyramid with the giant eyeball on it that glares at you? Well, for your information, that all-seeing eye is one of the great "Wonders of the World." It is an idol to mothers everywhere. It is one of the wonders of the world because everyone in the world wonders how in the heck Mom knew and saw what he or she would have sworn *no one* knew or saw!

Now, stay calm and hang in there; it gets a little sticky at this point. In my educated opinion, that eerie eyeball symbolizes the spirit of your mother and my mother. That eyeball is me, and, if you are a mother, that eyeball is you.

We mothers are like hawks. I tell you what, I see everything! It's like I have eyes in the back of my head.

My kids can't stand the fact that their mom is part alien. You see, when they were younger, I told them that I was from another planet — a planet where parents can see every activity a child does, no matter where they are. Worse than that, on this planet a child's thoughts are revealed to his parents through strange and cryptic images.

Steven, my youngest child, still believes me!

Mothers are like owls perched on a tree branch, hovering over the home — turning in every direction, seeing from every angle. Personally, I love hovering and hooting; I do it very well. Occasionally, I become the screech owl. When that happens, feathers fly!

She Watches!

Watching over the ways of your household is an incredible undertaking. Being watchful demands a calculated and concentrated effort in order to stay aware of every detail.

I suppose watching over the ways of one's household is parallel to planning a trip to outer space: You set your course; you think you know the what and where of the trip; but you never really know what's out there. I also liken this detailed profession of motherhood to that of a mathematician, scientist, or inventor.

You see, this is no light matter we are discussing. Motherhood and parental duty is at times like straining a muscle. Giving birth was easier and less painful. To be made stewards over lives and to be responsible for the

quality of those lives — this is the most sobering of all Heaven's delegated earthly duties.

So often when night comes, the worn-out mom, frazzled from the days events, has to forego her much-anticipated "alone time" to cool a fevered brow, soothe a heart in need of comfort, or help with homework that is past due. Oh, bread of idleness, how yummy you sound!

> **She watches over the ways of her household, and does not eat the bread of idleness.**
> **— Proverbs 31:27**

Remember, this virtuous woman watches. That involves waiting, and waiting involves wisdom. The fact that she opens her mouth with "wisdom" reveals that she has cultivated a life of waiting for the right moment. She knows how to watch and what to look for.

So many moms and dads have no idea what to look for. They have no idea what it means to watch over the ways of a household.

For one thing, watching is not spying. It is not gawking nor judging. Watching is *protecting* those you love from harmful predators. It is being sensitive to the air around you and your loved ones and learning how to rightly discern the spirit of a matter.

The American Heritage College Dictionary defines *to watch* this way:[14] 1) To observe carefully or continuously; 2) To look and wait expectantly or in anticipation; 3) To be on the lookout or alert ; to guard; 4) To stay awake deliberately;

keep vigil; 5) To keep up on and informed about; 6) To keep a watchful eye on; to tend.

Lord, Give Me Eyes To See

I know business people who are good friends with some of the "top dogs" of the executive world. These financial giants are soaring up the corporate ladder at the speed of light. How do they do it? They are blessed with financial acumen and have a very watchful eye on the economy. They know how to look for trends.

You have heard it said of people that "they have an eye for that." Whether it is art, bargains of all kinds, or real estate — you name it, there is someone out there who has an eye for it.

Well, there are also those who have a keen sense for business. It is a gift, and I respect these people's particular skill.

Yet, at the same time, many of these Wall Street wonders don't have a clue about what is going on with their own children. They have no idea why the son who was once so loving is now filled with anger or why the daughter who used to sit on Daddy's lap never leaves her room.

How sad and simple is the truth. We have focused in on the obvious, the surface, and the physical while the deeper and weightier things of heart and soul became neglected. We have had a superficial eye in our watching, and we have paid dearly for it.

Pulling Back the Curtain, Seeing Behind the Scenes

Let me share with you something that happened to my daughter Brittany when she was nine years old.

My daughter's school was forty-five minutes away, so she rode the bus each day. Each day on her return trip home, there was approximately fifteen minutes that she sat alone on the bus with a twelve-year-old boy.

He "seemed" (and as we know, not all things are as they seem) like a nice boy. Brittany mentioned him often.

One day when Brittany came home from school, something was different about her. When she entered the house, I could see she was not alone; a bad attitude had walked in with her.

My little girl was upset. I could see something was simmering inside her. I had that gut feeling that wrong had been done. A presence of condemnation was on Brittany, and where there is condemnation and guilt (if not released), there is anger.

It only took a moment for me to discern the situation. I asked, "Honey, what happened?" Brittany broke down crying.

I felt nervous, thinking she may have been molested. I fought off that inner sickening ache and prepared not to fall apart. I reminded myself that faith is the refusal to panic, but not a refusal to feel. I told myself to stay calm.

Thank God, Brittany wasn't physically molested, but the "nice" boy on the bus did molest her emotionally. He spoke perverted words to her. He asked if he could touch her, and then he talked filthy to her. Despite the fact that Brittany was all alone on that bus with the boy, she had enough courage to tell him no and that he was sick.

So Paul and I dealt with the situation. We hugged our daughter and prayed with her, binding the devil's strategy to harm her. Then with Brittany's okay, we went to the boy's house (we don't have time to get into that one). There was no shouting, no yelling, just dealing directly with this young man in front of his mother and father.

When the boss lady who supervises the school buses heard about this incident, she went bonkers! Oh, my! We all ran for cover. She was righteously angry, like an angel in the Old Testament standing by ready to strike.

This bus supervisor is a wonderful, straightforward, to-the-point, do-it-my-way type of woman. She looks at you, and you jump. She is tough, kind, and Catholic. Let me tell you something, my brother or sister, you don't mess with a good Catholic — especially one from Spain!

The lady took action. For starters, she kicked "Mr. Nice Guy" off the bus for the rest of the year. Then *pronto* she marched Paul and me and this kid into the guidance counselor's office at school.

There we were — Paul, me, the counselor, and this "nice," frightened little jerk. He didn't look so cool anymore. To stay in school, he had to see the counselor twice a week, along with other stipulations.

Brittany was happy we dealt with the situation so calmly yet aggressively. We were on her side, and she knew it.

Stupid devil! When Satan tries to mess with my daughter, Heaven gets involved. And when Heaven gets involved, the bad guy gets caught, convicted, and brought to the counselor's office! A little righteous butt-kicking is in order in that situation (figuratively speaking, of course).

You may think I'm talking crude. But let me assure you, when it comes to your children, you better intervene and get right in the face of any person who has wrong intentions. If you know about something off-color that has happened and you ignore it, you are allowing the devil to torment your little one.

I am not saying to shoot the sucker. I'm not telling you to slap the person or to call them on the phone cursing. But you should confront the problem in a godly way. Get involved, because the next advance may not be so easy to mend. You have to teach your children to be wise. But when they are still young, you cannot expect them to be their own defense.

She Watches Over Her Household's Ways

Brittany felt unclean, even though she did nothing wrong. "Sweetheart," I said, "let it go. You have not been a bad girl. You did not cause this."

"Then why do I feel so dirty?" Brittany asked, with the teary eyes of a nine-year-old who wonders why.

I explained, "You feel dirty because that boy and his filth got thrown all over you. His contaminating words brought this yucky feeling. Come here, Darling." Then we embraced and prayed, and love washed all the dirty feelings away.

If I had not been sensitive to "watch over the ways of my household" that day, I would not have seen the real problem. I would have only seen a child coming home from school with a rotten attitude. I would have attacked in the natural the problem I could see and hear, which would have closed the door for me to deal with the real, invisible problem hiding underneath.

Jesus said, *"...Be wise as serpents and harmless as doves"* (Matt. 10:16). Why a serpent? What wisdom can we learn from a slithering snake, of all things?

When you understand the word *serpent* as it pertains to this verse, you will clearly see Jesus' meaning. The word *serpent* here is the Greek word *ophis,* meaning "to give the idea of sharpness of vision."[15] When we cultivate sharpness of vision, we are wise.

That's what the Proverbs 31 woman does. *"...She watches over the ways of her household."* Her vision is sharp. She sees the way the home is headed. She sees the character development of each family member. She knows that each individual's character will propel the vessel (the family) in a certain direction, as does the rudder of a ship.

If the ways of her household are wrong, the course taken will be wrong. This mother knows that destinies are at stake. She realizes that family members cannot fulfill their destinies if they are off course. Therefore, she will not

tolerate a wayward vessel, for it will only result in wayward lives.

And what about the mother who does *not* watch over the ways of her family? It does not take a prophet to predict the heartache that is ahead. So much weeping waits around the corner for the mom who has never trained herself in the discipline of detection — the quieting of the emotions to clearly see the situation at hand.

To watch over the ways of your household, you have to be objective. You have to look at your own children realistically and see your own family honestly. You cannot guide them or protect them if you view them as faultless. If you think every child but *yours* has problems, your vessel is headed for destruction.

Our Families Are Like Gardens

The garden and its soil is a parable of the family. The success of any garden rests in understanding the basic needs of your garden. Be a good gardener, and life will bloom.

We purchase *Gardening Made Easy* books to teach us how to grow a breathtakingly beautiful and pleasant garden. The first thing we learn from these books is what tools are essential. For instance, essential tools may include:

- Spades
- Hand weeders
- Dutch hoe
- Three-bladed hoe
- Trimming and pruning tools
- Shears

- Edging irons
- Lawn rakes of all shapes

Now we test our soil, which must be healthy and full of nutrients to grow a garden. The soil is the womb, the incubator for all other plant life. Healthy soil is serious business.

My mom and I love to look at pictures of beautiful gardens. I once sent her a cute pop-up garden book showing ten different garden schemes with simple and easy directions to follow (yeah, right!).

These gardens, drawn on cardboard, were a happy mixture of the loveliest flowers I had ever seen. The colors and contrasts were spectacular.

For most of us, growing a garden like the ones the book depicted is a fantasy. In reality, the maintenance cost alone would be equivalent to most rent payments! And the time factor demands more attention than most of us can allot.

So what's a disgruntled gardener to do? Keep it small, simple, and maintainable. Enjoy those five healthy potted plants you have. And if you must have that flower garden, start out slow. Like everything else in life, enjoy what you have. Don't be heavy-hearted about what you don't have nor will ever have.

And will you do me a favor? I beg you, please don't become so desperate for a flower garden that you insult nature and your neighbors by sticking hundreds of fake plastic flowers out in the dirt. A few fake flowers won't hurt, but be selective and sly about it. Please protect the reputation of all garden lovers everywhere!

The Nitty-Gritty About Gardens

**(About Families, Raising Children,
Being Organized, Getting Homework Done...)**

Raising a family and growing a garden are both experiences that can be likened unto a war zone. The gardener silently stalks, fighting pests, killing those nasty leaf-eaters and floral-feasters. The trick is to destroy the pest without destroying the lovely Clematis or Cornus Alba you have so painstakingly cultivated. But the truth is, if you *don't* kill the pests, they will eat your entire garden, roots and all.

Every garden has weeds, including the garden of your family. That's why you must continually be on the lookout for weedy intruders.

I could go on and on. The point is that gardening is a lot of work — rewarding, wonderful, back-breaking, dirt-under-the-fingernails work.

There are so many different kinds of parasites just waiting to get their hooks into the healthy garden of your family. Just when you think your garden is immune — guess what? They rear their ugly heads again. Weeds and parasites are like the return of some scary movie in which the ominous intruders boast, *"We're back!"*

All your work and toil will be wasted if you do not tend to the garden daily. Be watchful, my friend.

This weed thing can really get to you if you don't understand the way of a garden. You just have to accept the fact that there will always be weeds to pull and pests to execute. If you are a gardener, it is one of your "always" tasks.

And the same is true in regard to your family. Each and every day, it is guaranteed that weeds will spring up overnight. Deadly weeds like doubt, worry, and strife are poisons that work hand in hand and side by side, just as faith, hope, and love work hand in hand and side by side.

But don't lose heart. As you diligently watch over your garden, something special begins to happen. The garden starts evolving and maturing. It starts to take care of itself little by little. The weeds become less and less troublesome. Those parasites, your antagonistic adversaries, have been brought under control. Truly you have taken dominion.

Your garden has been so well taken care of that it now responds almost artistically to the care that you give it. Each work of art blooms in its own place. Yes, the work of a gardener is never completed, but the garden does start revealing a reward for all your effort.

A mature garden is a joy to be around. And so it shall be with our families.

Chapter Sixteen

Such a 'Crumby' Life!

...And [she] *does not eat the bread of idleness.*

— Proverbs 31:27

*N*ow, about that bread. You know, the bread of idleness — or is it the loaf of laziness? Anyway... Hey, I know! We could start a new bakery and café for all the idle moms who find it totally horrible to have to run a home.

You've probably met some of these women. They have dirty laundry all over the house and dirty dishes piled up in the bathtub. The children are unkempt, and Mom sits in front of the television watching "America's Most Sleazy" — those low-life, no-life, expose-it-all talk shows.

All the while, this same woman swears on a stack of Bibles that she has no time to get anything done. She is idle. Why she is idle, I'm not sure. More than likely, depression

has set in, and she cannot find the strength needed to rise up and fulfill her household responsibilities. Something has taken the wind out of her sails.

We can help her, you and I. Jesus will teach her through us that taking care of a home and a family can be a joy. We can encourage her to find reason and purpose in Christ. We can teach her how to be a good mother. However, she must be open. Only if she will open up to us can we help.

I realize that there are some stubborn moms out there. Often they are women who are angry at the way their life has turned out, and they make darn sure everyone who crosses their path knows about their sour life.

This type of woman is not thrilled with the home life to begin with. The entire idea of all this Proverbs 31, make-yourself-a-better-mother-and-wife stuff makes her very uncomfortable.

Not only does this kind of woman eat the bread of idleness, she also "kneads" it to survive. Her time is spent in perfecting the recipe. She senses that if she ever stopped eating this bread of idleness (or it could also be called "the bread of blame"), she would have to take a deep breath and grow up and be responsible.

'More Pits, Please'

Let's see, what could we do for these ladies? I got it! They need to visit this café I used to eat at regularly. The waitress knew me by name, and I knew the menu by heart.

As I remember, this café (in which I own stock) had a specialty line of *"attitude delights"* — treats such as Murmuring Muffins and Bitterness Bread (using sourdough, of course!). The menu was impressive! Featured in the "sad-wich" section, such delicacies as the following were offered:

- "Bad Attitude on Hole Wheat," loaded with pickles and lemons (I've choked on that one before!)
- The "Half-Hearted Ham" served on dry rye
- "Peanut Butter and Jealousy" (Oh, dear!)
- The famous "B-L-T" ("Board-Lazy and Testy")
- The "Really Rude Reuben" (I eat that while I'm driving in Manila traffic!)
- The "Suffering Submarine" (Guaranteed to depress you with every bite!)
- The "Nobody Loves Me Knockwurst"

To my recollection, the café had only one salad: the "Woe Is Me Waldorff." That was my unfortunate favorite. Then when I was nauseatingly full, the waitress would entice me with Sybarite Supreme, topped with prune and cherry pits. My flesh was already in a state of complete emotional indulgence, so I'd think, *Why stop now?*

Yes, I remember that restaurant well. Praise God, I haven't eaten there for years. I've driven by at times; I've even been tempted to stop and go in. It's a cozy-looking place, but I've always left it with an upset stomach and a heavy heart. Thank God, I've been delivered!

If you have been eating at this café — run! Get up and get out of there before you feel like you belong there. Something weird happens to you at that café. The food

becomes addictive and starts to work on all your senses, changing the way you see things.

My advice? First, after getting the heck out of there, *go home*. Then once you're home, *make* it a home. Gather your children and give them each a big hug. (The value of hugs is certainly underestimated!) Next, look those children right in the eyes and see through to their hearts. See how much they need you. Even more importantly, see how much they love you. Every day of their lives, they look to you for assurance that in your arms and in your care, everything is going to be all right.

But before you can ever make your house a home, you have to get out of that café.

Do Unto Them...

I don't always live up to Jesus' admonition in Matthew 7:12 to "do unto others as you would have others do unto you." However, fulfilling that commandment is my life's pursuit — right after the greatest commandment, "Thou shalt love the Lord your God with all your heart, soul, mind, and strength" (Mark 12:30). What other verses are there? Those two cover it all — end of sermon.

My point is this: Think of how you would want to be treated if you were a child, and then treat your children accordingly.

I understand that you may not be living in the best of circumstances. And granted, your life may not have turned out the way you had dreamed. If that is true, I'm so sorry — so sincerely sorry.

But even so, please understand that the neglect you felt or still feel can be passed down in so many ways. Neglected homes and neglected hearts so often go together.

Just as you have cried out, wanting to be heard and helped, your children also cry out. They cry out to you for a home that is not only clean and somewhat in order, but decorated with bright colors of comfort — a home where each room is painted with love, laughter, and lots of big, fluffy pillows of peace.

So now what? What can you do? Where can you go from here? There must be a way to go forward from this seemingly impassable point.

There is. Once and for all, you can leave that awful café where you may have taken up residence. You can change your eating habits and stop eating the bread of idleness. Instead, you can feast on God's Word, where love and forgiveness flavor every aspect of life and mercy is never out of season.

God's Word is my new menu from which I now choose to continually eat. I invite you to come dine with me. I'll introduce you to Jesus, and He will introduce you to the Father. And what happens then? Well, let me just say that once you know the Father, there is nothing left *to* say — only a life with Him to experience.

You Will Need a Friend

So take my hand. I believe we can go together to this place — a place so close to God, so very near to His promises of hope and healing, that we will actually be able

to grasp them. (That's right — I said *we*. You'll need a friend to help you along the way.)

Whatever may have caused you to eat the bread of idleness, let it go — whether the cause is a deep disappointment, shattered expectations and dreams, or wounds so deeply inflicted on your heart that release seems impossible.

Let it go. *Refuse* bitterness. If you don't, bitterness will fill the very air you breathe. Before long, you will start to inhale its fumes. Then you will discover just how toxic bitterness is, not only to you but to those around you.

But you don't have to inhale those poisonous fumes. You can breathe in the very breath of life.

> **And the Lord God formed man of the dust of the ground, and breathed into his nostrils the breath of life; and man became a living soul.**
>
> **— Genesis 2:7**

In the beginning, God created man, forming life and purpose out of the dust. Then He gave man breath, and, thus, He gave him life.

God did it once, and He will do it again — in *you*.

Chapter Seventeen

They Call Her the Loveliest of Names

Her children rise up and call her blessed; her husband also, and he praises her.

— Proverbs 31:28

*A*ll women are great, but moms are even greater people. Hopefully, we've established those facts beyond any reasonable doubt. But have we established the fact that a mom's brains are similar to a pulsating computer and that with each breath she takes, a calendar of events spews out spontaneously?

Moms know how to put life in order. Most of the time, they schedule life well, planning events far in advance (unless they are eating that bread of idleness, that is!). Many of them are beyond organized — they hinge on being neurotic. They have already scheduled the high school prom

night — even though their beloved daughter is still in the third grade!

I mean, a mom thinks about everything, and her children see that. They have seen for years what mom has accomplished. And most of what she has accomplished has been for them.

That's why "her children rise up and bless her."

Dear me, they ought to! These kids aren't fools. They know a good thing when they see it, and they see a good thing in their mom. They know that not all moms are like their mom. They've talked with their friends; they know that some moms don't stick around. They're well aware of the home life around the corner.

These children understand a basic sowing and reaping principle here. They think, *We need to give back to this woman who gives so much to us.*

And what can a child give to a mom? *Appreciation.* Just a little gratitude goes such a long way. It is life energizing, this "kids' song of praise." It is the fuel needed to continue to bless and want to bless.

How Excellent Is Your Name, O Mom!

Our strength is zapped when we give to thankless adults and bratty kids. That shouldn't stop our giving; after all, we are good moms. But let's be honest — no matter how good we want to be, there are times when we want to snap, snarl, and tell our ungrateful loved ones, "Get your

own #@! breakfast!" But we don't (or maybe we do!), and eventually love once again takes over.

When we feel unappreciated, the heart forces a smile, but it is tinged with heaviness. I know that our giving should be unto the Lord and that we are to give as if we were giving to Him. But within our immediate family, we need to both hear and say those most cherished words, "Thank you."

When I give and give and then give some more, it hurts when all my giving is belittled and trampled on. In the past, I have reacted to such ingratitude like an offended child, pouting and sulking, holding back love. How foolish! How can one hold back that which he or she was created to do — to love, bless, and give to others?

We adults also need to grow up and realize that selfishness is a huge part of childhood. Heck, what am I saying? It's a huge part of adulthood! We humans are basically selfish and stingy — some more than others. (I'm sure, dear reader, that you, like me, deal with that wonderful flesh attribute on a daily basis!) God help us all!

They Arise and Call Her Blessed

It is so interesting to me that her sons and daughters wake up and call her *blessed*. They christen her with a title, conveying what they have seen in her.

They call her what she is. They call her what she does.

It is as if this is their prayer: "Oh, blessed Mom, be blessed still. Be blessed with all you have done. May it all come back your way."

"They rise up." Mom is not having to jerk them out of bed screaming and hollering. *They* miraculously get up, and right away the kiddies start speaking niceties!

I have never allowed my children to wake up mean. If they do, I march them right back to bed and have them start over. It is far too easy to begin the day at odds with the world. Any "flesh blob" (obviously this refers to someone who is *not* a Spirit-led person!) can wake up cranky.

I always start my mornings with the children by saying, "Wake up, sweethearts. Wake up, guys. Say 'Good morning' to the Lord." That has become my ritual and a daily routine.

If that doesn't work, however, I resort to Plan B. Plan B is when the screaming and cover-grabbing begins. I momentarily and conveniently forget my dignity, along with my Christianity.

Wearing full battle gear, with cudgel in hand, I come prepared for the war to begin. I engage the enemy by first disrupting their coziness. Second, I leave them (the enemy) half-naked in a freezing, air-conditioned room (if it's summer) with five one-hundred-watt light bulbs beaming. These specially made bulbs are guaranteed to cause a glare that temporarily blinds the unfortunate sluggard who dared to doze an extra minute.

Don't worry; I don't think the special light bulbs cause any permanent damage. My children have informed me that by midday, normal sight returns. However, I *have* heard that in some cases, the pupils' ability to dilate is never quite the same.

But, by golly, those kids learn! Now filled with wisdom and insight, they know that when my melodious voice echoes down the hallway the next morning, they better get up! And, God bless their darling hearts, they do!

('Mornin', Mom')

Her children call her a name — and it's a good one. *The American Heritage College Dictionary* describes *bless* and *blessed* this way: "to honor; to glorify; to invoke divine favor upon; to confer well-being upon; enjoying happiness; fortunate; bringing happiness."[16]

According to the *Strong's Concordance,* the Hebrew word *blessed* is *aw-shar.* Used in the widest sense, it means "to be level, right, happy; to go forward; to be honest; to prosper."[17] Gee, and all I get in the morning is a half-blinded, squinting child who slurs unintelligibly, "◆❊□□■✝■♍ ◆❊□○."

Translation, I realize, is needed. From the various fonts offered on my computer, that was "Wingdings" for "Mornin', Mom."

I do not understand why "Wingdings" is even offered on my computer, or on anyone else's for that matter. This could be a subversive plot. Is there a program I can purchase to learn decoding? Is there a sector of our society that uses "Wingdings" in communicating? If so, I don't think I want to meet them. They probably are good friends with those who use the "Marlett" font: "❑ ⁄⁄ ⁄⁄ ⌐ ■ ✕ • ⌐ ⌐!" (That was "Good grief!" Marlett style!)

'Mommy, You Are Great, We Bless You, We Bless You...'

Now about my kids.

I have pondered long and hard, and I believe it's time I gave my children some lessons on blessing "dear ol' Mommy."

Most of us are accustomed to hearing "God bless you" only after we have sneezed all over the sorry sap standing too close to us. And that type of blessing (although I don't think it qualifies as a real blessing) is only said out of elementary good manners.

This is what the person *really* wants to say: "Man, what a pig. Go take your sick self home and quit infecting the rest of healthy society with your stupid cold!" That's not exactly the kind of blessing I am talking about!

My children have never spoken out a decree of good will upon me, not the way the children of this virtuous mother have. My children don't curse me either; I just never hear blessings like I mentioned earlier.

Now, Star Trek's "Mr. Spock" was raised correctly. His family's motto was "Live long and prosper." Since people from their planet were devoid of emotion, they didn't feel anything when they said that to each other. But it must have been nice to hear it nonetheless.

Can you imagine hearing your children greet you at breakfast like this? "Good morning, Mother. I confer well-being upon you this fine day. Good morning, Father

Fortunate and Mother Happiness. May you prosper and go forward."

After hearing such unfamiliar words to our ears, we may at first think that our children have just smarted off to us. We might even lean over and twist somebody's lips, demanding an explanation!

But after a while, we just might to get used to the way such a nice greeting sounds. Then, as the children go off to school, we'll begin to say back to them, "May divine favor be yours!"

Hey, it has a pleasant ring to it!

'Her Husband Also, and He Praises Her'

Her husband also. Do you hear that, O male reader of mine? Shall we read once more this eternal passage? It says that much honor is given and expressed in this home for Mom.

And where is Dad? He is smack dab right in the middle of it all, adding his praise for his wife to the rest of the family's tribute. How well they all harmonize!

> **Her children rise up and call her blessed; her husband also, and he praises her.**
> **— Proverbs 31:28**

For years the husband has seen all his wife has accomplished, and most of it has been for the family. He knows a good thing when he sees it, and he sees a good thing in her. He knows that not all wives are like his wife. He realizes that

some wives don't stick around. He talks with his friends; he is well aware of the home life around the corner.

He understands a basic seedtime-and-harvest principle here, so he thinks, *I need to give back to this woman who gives so much to me.* And what can he give her? *Appreciation.* Just a little gratitude goes a long way.

Haven't I said all this somewhere before? Well, it still sounds good — real good!

Chapter Eighteen

Forever a Daughter

"Many daughters have done well, but you excel them all."

— Proverbs 31:29

I have written so much about this Proverbs 31 woman. My intent has been to exemplify and illustrate all I can concerning this working wife, mother, and stabilizing force of the family.

Until now, we have spotlighted her as a mom and as a helpmate. But she is not only a wife and a mother; she is also a *daughter.*

I am a daughter and a sister. Before I ever became a wife and mother, I was and forever will be a daughter and a sister.

You and I are so many people. We incur so many titles as we live our lives, and each title invites a different response depending on the responsibility it entails.

I am a daughter. I am a sister. I am an auntie. I am a sister-in-law. I am a wife. I am a mother. I am a minister. I am a friend. I am, hopefully, *not* an enemy. That is just to list the few of the persons I am, without even mentioning the responsibilities I have with each title.

I am a daughter. I like the sound of that. Not only am I a daughter, I am to fulfill my responsibilities as a daughter. That means I have a mommy somewhere. I have a daddy somewhere. And to those two still-living parents, I have some giving to do.

I am to bless and do good to those two special people in my life. I am to reach out to them, to love and honor them, to somehow make them happy. Not only *am* I a daughter, but I am to *be* a daughter.

I especially love being a daughter to my mom. I enjoy blessing her. I get a kick out of spoiling her. She wears the prettiest smile when she's at peace.

I have taken it upon myself to make her life easier and a little bit more meaningful, and that has turned in my favor. Blessing her has made my life more meaningful.

Certainly I love my dad too; I just don't know him as well as I do my mom. They divorced when I was twelve, and from that point on, my dad and I were like related strangers. Since the divorce, I have not had him in my life, yet he has always found a place in my heart. He has not walked with me most of my life, yet his and my prayers do join hands.

I have no memory of Daddy teaching me or instructing me while I was growing up. Now that I am older and have lived in Asia for so many years, time and distance has made it difficult to have many "dinners at Dad's house." But when my family goes home during the summers, I see Dad for a few days and enjoy those brief moments immensely.

Daddy's Little Girl, All Grown Up

I believe that relationships that could not be restored on earth because of lost years will be made new in Heaven. Even relationships will be "born again." Therefore, I believe that in Heaven, I will one day have a close relationship with Daddy that I never had on earth.

My father is a saved man now. There are so many miracles God has in store for us. The Savior said, "Behold, I make all things new" (Rev. 21:5). I love my dad and I bless him — although I really don't know him. Our lives have journeyed far from each other.

I am not suggesting it's easy to bless a father whom you haven't known or to bless a mom who has been far in heart from you. On the contrary, it isn't easy. And if they have hurt you, it is never easy, especially if blessing them is the farthest thing from your mind. You may have been thinking a little more in line with cursing them, resenting them, or at best tolerating them, but certainly not blessing them.

Maybe your dad walked away from the family. Maybe he was around but neglected you. Or perhaps the unthinkable happened — he abused you. Then again, maybe it was Mom who walked out on the family. There are so many sad scenarios, so much sorrow in so many people's stories.

I won't play the part of the psychologist, just the preacher. I would not want to speak in such a calculated way about your grief, since I know so little about the brutal facts that changed the course of your emotions forever. To speak with some sort of authority in so few lines might make it seem like I trivialize and minimize the ache that has become a part of you. I would never want to come across so cold and self-assured.

I hurt inside as I write this portion of my book. I cry for you who have felt abandoned and for you who have been abandoned. You who have had terrible parents, I am so sorry. I do have pity, but even more that that, I have a prayer — for the wound that oozes still, for the heart pain that will not heal.

If only the legendary drug of ancient times *nepenthe* were real. It was said to ease suffering and sorrow. But in this natural world, there is nothing yet known as a remedy for grief. Only our God, only the Healer, can touch the emotions and truly heal.

Oh, Jesus, help those who are still so bruised, I sincerely pray.

Yet you are still a daughter. You have within you the power to start a new cycle of love. You can begin doing what daughters should do, irrespective of what you never received from your own parents (this applies to sons, too, of course). As a child now grown, you can forgive; you can pray; you can try to rebuild. It is your turn to set the record straight.

I can be what my parents may never have been. I am still a daughter, regardless of their actions.

Forgiveness Lets Your Life Move Forward — With a Smile!

Let me ease some of the pressure you may be feeling concerning forgiveness. First, forgiveness is not as difficult as you may have thought. A life of forgiving and loving is much easier than a life of bitterness and hatred.

Forgiveness is *not* forgetting. No one completely forgets emotional and physical agony. Forgiving is also not calling your enemy and throwing a party for him just to prove you're free.

The verse that says, "Love your enemy" (Matt. 5:44) has been used as a weapon to accuse people who have been wronged of not loving enough. However, the Greek word for *love* in this passage of Scripture simply means "to be social with; civil."[18]

Forgiveness begins when you come to understand that God will work in the lives of those who have hurt you. Forgiveness demands one thing — that you turn it over to the Lord. Whatever and whoever has hurt you, give it to God.

The first step toward forgiveness is to become concerned with your own heart's condition. When you walk in forgiveness, you will find yourself praying for your adversary, knowing that only a touch from the Lord will stop the pain both you and he or she feels.

Now that I am all grown up, I stand before the Lord representing myself, not my parents. My life will speak for

itself. I do not speak for another's life. I do not condemn or carry others' mistakes.

The Lord sees the daughter I am. When it is all over, the final word will be His. He will judge who was and who was not what they should have been. Until that time, I am and must be a daughter.

Mom: My Forever-and-Ever Friend

Of all the gifts given me, none is like my mother, Donna May. When Dad and she divorced, Mom was there for us every step of the way. I will never forget how hard she worked.

She became an unskilled laborer. My older sister was already out of the house, working and struggling to make it on her own, trying hard to find some meaning in all the madness. At home remained my brother Steve, my sister Stacy, and me. We were close and had good times, although Mom had days of depression that would take its toll years later.

It became a normal part of our lives to watch our mom constantly wrestle the foe of finances day after day and year after year. Life hadn't turned out the way Mom had dreamed. She married young and gave birth to four children, besides having several miscarriages. Then after nearly dying from polio, she was left handicapped by the disease at the vibrant age of thirty. Life was looking pretty grim. For someone who had loved ice skating, running, dancing, and being active, learning to walk all over again was not easy.

Mom lived through twenty years of marriage to an alcoholic husband who had turned abusive. Afterwards, there

were many days she waited in welfare lines to receive a check. None of this was the picture Donna May had painted for her life. Certainly there was no fairy-tale ending here.

However, despite it all, my mom was a good mom. She cooked great meals, kept a beautiful home, was kind and compassionate, and she got involved with our little lives.

How drastically different the beginning and the end of a story can be. The pages of decisions called everyday life, along with a few chapters of tragedy, can affect our "happy-ever-afters" forever.

Page after page from Mom's life is scripted in bold, tragic letters — that is, until Jesus came to live with us. Then He began to change everything.

My parents were not Christians when I was growing up, so a lot went on that was not "righteous." But Mom was still good. My father could have been good; he just didn't know how to handle life with all of its pressures. So he did what many without God do when faced with life's pressures: he fell into sin and drank.

My dad's sin cost him dearly, but years later he did find God. He sobered up and began living for the Lord. His life turned into a wonderful testimony of the Lord's graciousness and forgiving mercy.

You Have One Earth Life — Treat It Kindly

Here's a sad and almost sacred truth to remember: *The life you waste is gone forever. Decisions and destinies go*

hand in hand, and there are ruined cities you can never rebuild.

The financial pressure on Mom was terrible. The pressure was on all of us, of course, but she bore the brunt of it. Working as a maid or a factory worker, Mom cried more tears than I will ever know.

I was not a kind, understanding daughter back then. I was angry and selfish and upset with the world. I was a teenager who had dreams, and no one was making those dreams come true for me. No one seemed to care in those days. Later I found out that many did care, but so few had the ability to change the things that needed changing.

I gave my life to Jesus when I was fifteen years old, along with Mom and my sister Stacy. One night all three of us asked the Savior to come into our hearts and be the Lord and Master of our lives. Steve and Steff were not living at home anymore, but a few years later they, too, would meet the Lord.

At seventeen, my heart went through some sort of spiritual surgery. God's initial incision cut deep. He told me I was selfish. He also said I was stingy.

When God speaks to you, you either shut your eyes tight or open them wide. I chose to open my eyes wide. And in this new wide-eyed vision, I saw my mom through a loving, tender heart.

I saw the woman I loved so much in a clear, compassionate way. I felt her pain and wanted nothing more than to ease some of that pain for her. I wanted to make her happy. Somehow and in some way, I wanted to give to her and bless her. I wanted to be one of the daughters who

made her laugh, gave her things, spoiled her a bit. Simply put, I wanted to take care of her. And why not? I am a daughter; I should *act* like a daughter.

Give and Give and Give (Bless and Bless and Bless), And You Will Never Lack!

Mom is blessed and happy now — not only because of *my* giving; that would be far from the truth. The giving of all her children has made her life joyful and less burdensome.

I still love to give to her. It has been said that when I come home, it's like Santa Claus coming to town! That is definitely exaggerated, although I wish I could afford it to be true. If I had the money — oh, the things I would do for that mom of mine! It just looks like I do a lot because I am only home in the summer, so I combine months' worth of giving into a short span of time. I want her to know that until her last breath, I will continue to breathe goodness upon her. She has a daughter in me who will always be there.

How blessed Mom is! She has three daughters and a son who all feel the same way. *I pray we have done well and excel them all in rising up and calling her blessed!*

Chapter Nineteen

Charmed, I'm Sure

Charm is deceitful and beauty is vain, but a woman who fears the Lord, she shall be praised.

— Proverbs 31:30

*C*harm is deceitful and beauty is vain? Within the core of these most descriptive words, could it be possible that evil lurks? In and of themselves, the words *charm* and *beauty* seem rather pleasant.

If your daughter is clumsy and continues to walk into walls and trip over her own shadow, charm and beauty school might be something to look into. Nothing objectionable strikes me as yet.

In tribute to the concepts of charm and beauty, my cinematic resources envision movies' classic ladies such as Audrey Hepburn, Katharine Hepburn, and Vivian Leigh.

The more innocent side of charm and beauty is seen in movies like "Little Women," "The Little Princess," "The Little Mermaid," and "Pollyanna." And we can't talk about charm and beauty without mentioning "Cinderella" (who, by the way, is a recognized saint in most religious circles!).

The young ladies depicted in these classics create an image of feminine charm. The only one who shows even a tinge of having an attitude is Ariel the little Mermaid. And who can blame her? She is tired of being half-fish and half-human!

But even though Ariel may not be "charming" at all times, she is certainly sincere, kind, and adventurous. And although she is also somewhat irresponsible, she is genuine. Yes, that's it — *she is genuine.*

Speaking of those genuine types, Anne with an "e" from the movie "Anne of Green Gables" is a perfect example. Anne, with all her rambunctious, never-a-dull-moment ways, is the epitome of the genuine in heart.

But then, that is Hollywood. Its characters are lifeless once the director says it's the final take.

Chen, the Hebrew word for "kindness, graciousness, and well-favored,"[19] interchanges with the word *charm* in many Bibles. These are fabulous adjectives to enhance one's description of a woman — "kindness, graciousness, and well-favored." Hopefully, they describe someone's recollection of you and me. (Wouldn't *that* be nice?)

Not All That Glitters Is Gold

Charm — see how it glitters? Be not deceived. As the old saying goes, "Not all that glitters is gold." From a distance,

iron pyrite or "fool's gold" dazzles. It can make one dizzy with determination, because a counterfeit seems to announce that the real thing is out there somewhere.

Fool's gold is radiant, blinding the novice treasure hunter. But if you want authenticity, stay away from it. Stay away from zirconium too. It's not that real diamond you've been saving for. Its lustrous illusion is crafted to trick and entice you.

That same advice applies to someone who only *seems* charming.

Now, don't misunderstand me; I like zirconium, and even more because it *is* fake. It's fun, fancy, and cheaper then the genuine. Fake is fine when it comes to jewelry.

On the other hand, fake is *not* fine when it comes to people. People who are fake are definitely cheaper to obtain and effortless to come by compared to genuine people. And can fake people dazzle you? You bet they can. So beware and be leery of those from the planet of "Zircon"!

When you know the difference between the fabricated and the factual, the signature brands and the pretty impostors, choosing a quality outfit or friend is made much easier because there is no deception blinding you.

Hopefully, we all have a little charm, but how we use our charm can sometimes be a bit ambiguous. And there lies the turning point — when the color of charm chances to fade. Manipulative motives hidden by a sweet smile only serve to twist situations. That's when charm gets a bad rap.

To have charm and to use it to be falsely alluring is where the word *charm* starts to digress. Back to my faithful

friend, *The American Heritage College Dictionary.* One of its definitions of *charm* is to "to cast or seem to cast a spell on; to act as if with magic."[20]

"She's so charming," a woman says of her friend's daughter. That comment could very well refer to a wonderful child.

Remember, charm is an outer act, not necessarily a reflection of inner attitudes. To be charming is to be publicly polished. That isn't a bad quality. But when that quality stands all alone — when it isn't matched with a God-pleasing heart condition — that is when we find the shallowness of charm.

It is far too easy to picture a "charming brat" — one who acts kind but is not. On the contrary, this socially soothing personality can be curt and cunning behind closed doors.

Life demands many performances, but how tiring to live that way, always performing for others. A charmer in front of the crowd invites attention and even awe. But behind the scene, a "charming" stage presence can reek with a sour attitude. Charm and beauty are *not* blood-related to being genuine.

Once we crack open this nebulous nut called charm and beauty, we find so little sincerity, truth, or integrity in it. We find so little faithfulness and inviting character traits.

Have you ever thought that charm and beauty would be hanging out with such a deceitful lot? Beauty has been defiling charm and vise versa for a long time. The two work well together because pride ignites their dark sides.

Proverbs 31:30 says that beauty is vain. Another translation says beauty is "passing." Maybe that is why we cling to it in a panic-like state. It's not around for very long. But it lingers long enough to corrupt and lead astray young men and women, tear families to shreds, and cloud up simple issues.

Yes, outer beauty is a goddess. And in the end all who worship her find absolute, top-of-the-line *emptiness and despair*! Why? Because beauty fades and passes away until her worshipper is left with nothing.

Our symposium's main speaker, Lemuel's mother, slows her ecstatic dialogue down to give her son a warning — indeed, to give us all a warning. She stops enumerating the countless qualities and duties of this prominent and prized woman to voice a concern. This half of a verse is the only part of the poem that deals with a negative. It's the only verse that flashes a red light. It's the only verse out of twenty-two verses where nothing is shared about what this woman does or how great she is.

Instead, a seven-word warning is given: "Charm is deceitful, and beauty is vain." We are no longer dealing with a living mentor; instead, we have now learned from these two very descriptive words, *charm* and *beauty*.

Beauty Is Vain

If it is honor you want and a little praise you need, *love God*. There is no earthly adoration man can give that compares to having God on your side. The thunder of human applause is meaningless if all is not well with your soul. Seeking God with all your heart will assure you a place at the world's table of business and opportunity. Don't worry —

being godly and educated, not gorgeous, will open doors for you.

A woman who puts God first will have a position in the corporate world if she so desires. She will have esteem, and she will have honor. You see, contrary to popular opinion, it is not the prettiest and the shapeliest who always capture the camera. Granted, there will always be the "horny hounds" out there who will only hire a woman if she looks like a candidate for a centerfold.

Oh, well! Forget them. Keep your head up high and your clothes on. Perfect your skill and keep sharpening your intelligence, and your gift will surely make room for you. You do not have to be a knock-out to win a place in history.

I was talking to my daughter recently about beauty. We discussed the malicious lie of it all, which claims that beauty is the only calling card to success.

I said, "Honey, think of all the great female singers you admire and then answer me this: Are they all beautiful? Is talent limited to looks? Is every actress you see in movies gorgeous? Is every doctor, lawyer, or businesswoman a model? Is every athlete, teacher, playwright, social worker or surgeon stunning in looks? The answer is certainly no!"

My daughter likes the magazine *Seventeen*. Okay, no big deal. Then I started reading it. I went page by page through the magazine with Brittany. "Look at this, Brittany!" I pointed out. "Not one girl in this entire 244-page magazine has a pimple or braces. There isn't one ugly guy, not one girl with a flat chest, not one fat or even one 'pleasantly' plump girl!"

The *Seventeen* issues I held in my hand did not have one article about career options. Not one article explained how to prepare for the future, how to be on the honor roll, how to have self-esteem, or how to stay positive in a negative world. Looks were everything. Boys and fashion were this magazine's printed priorities.

How vulnerable our young are, how impressionable and in need of acceptance!

That's why Proverbs 31:30 is so important when it says, *"...a woman who fears the Lord, she will be praised."*

Why will this woman be praised or admired? Because she is a woman of great confidence and courage. She is a woman of her word, a woman of wisdom and understanding. She can be trusted. That aura attracts both people and positions.

So, of course, go ahead and fix yourself up. That is a given. But make sure you focus in on the whole picture of life — a picture that includes the fat, the not-so-pretty, and the clumsy.

And whoever you are — enjoy life. Enjoy knowing the Lord. Laugh a lot, sing a lot, and be beautiful on the inside, and the outside will shine *radiantly.*

Chapter Twenty

Whatever a Man Sows, That He Will Reap

Give her of the fruit of her hands, and let her own works praise her in the gates.

— Proverbs 31:31

*W*ell, we've made it! The trip is nearly over. You have done so well. You rarely stumbled. On *my* first trek through Proverbs 31, you couldn't count the falls, the constant scrapes, and the toe-stubbed walks I endured. You're tougher and more teachable than I thought! When we met, you looked quite frightened, but I guess there was a warrior deep inside after all.

You're a person who has longed to travel to a place not previously traveled before. Your heart has taken you to a

different level now. I promised you would never be the same, and so it has happened.

Here we find ourselves visiting the final verse concerning "the life and times" of this famed female we have grown to admire. We stand gazing at the closing statements — and then the book closes.

For me, your beloved guide, this is the verse of all verses. That is appropriate, for the best is traditionally saved for last. This verse will linger when the others get lost in the far reaches of our memories. This one will be savored, for it has been simmering — well, for thirty long verses!

Instruction has died down, and a diploma of sorts is given. This verse is the culmination of all the doing already done.

It is this woman's reaping time, her "due season." The Lord of the harvest has clearly stated, *"And let us not grow weary while doing good, for IN DUE SEASON WE SHALL REAP if we do not lose heart"* (Gal. 6:9).

It is truly her "dew" season. The field called her life has been watered well, and harvest time is here. She has sown, and now she shall reap.

Clear and simple.

Without dispute, without any debate, there is a debt to be paid to this godly woman. So just as the earth yields a harvest from seeds sown within her soil, now Heaven yields out of its abundance. From all that this one fruitful life has sown, she now receives her reward.

Her Due Season

This due season we speak of is the law of life and the law of Heaven.

You see, there are about twenty-three *she* statements in Proverbs 31 that point to seeds sown. Let's look at some of them: "She does him good"; "She seeks wool"; "She willingly works"; "She brings"; "She rises"; "She provides"; "She considers"; "She girds"; "She perceives"; "She stretches out her hands"; "She is not afraid"; "She makes"; "She opens"; and "She watches."

All that doing involves a lot of seed sowing! We know that to be true, for throughout this book, we have observed page after page of this woman's lifetime of sowing. No doubt, if we continued to keep track of her life, we'd also observe a lifetime of much reaping.

All of our doings are seeds sown as well. (Thank God, we are talking here about *good* seeds!) So when will that "due season" come? I don't know. It belongs to God. He owns the "when" and "where," the "for whom" and the "how much."

I can tell you from experience, though, that the "due season" is fun!

1. It is constant and spontaneous.
2. It is around the corner.
3. It comes when you least expect it.
4. It comes when you don't think you deserve it.
5. It does not come when you think you do.
6. It is big when you think you should get a little.

7. And sometimes it is little when you think you should get lots.

This due season is based on a system we know so little about. It is based on purity of heart, forgiveness, and faith. It is based on the knowledge of God's promises. It is based on prayer.

A Lifestyle of Giving

But you can do all the things I just mentioned and still be lacking. The truth is, you will live in lack until you learn to be a giver, until you learn how to be a wise farmer who knows that no harvest is reaped without sowing.

> **Give her the fruit of her hands....**
> — **Proverbs 31:31**

Go ahead and let her be blessed; she has earned it!

I have had people marvel at the blessings that have come my way. I, too, marvel with gratitude but not with shock. I knew when I decided to be a giver years ago that I eventually would reap.

When Paul and I graduated from Bible school, our commencement speaker was T. L. Osborn. What a fabulous meal Dr. Osborn served us that day, fresh and piping hot, full of nutrition for the spirit!

Out of that great message, I remembered this statement the most: "If you make others happy, you will be happy. If you bless others, you will be blessed. If you make others rich, you will be rich — so *go forth...*"

And so we did. We went forth preaching and teaching, doing what missionaries do best. And to this day, that's what we continue to do.

But in my quiet times, alone and away from the ministry, I would have my own private talks with God about what I had heard from our graduation speaker. I told the Lord I wanted to accept that challenge of developing the lifestyle of a giver.

So that's what I did. And, my friend, that has proven to be the greatest, the most rewarding part of my life. Aside from living a life of praise and prayer, giving has showed me the heart of my Father more than anything else.

I have learned that one cannot outgive God. He sees everything we do, and, further, He sees everything we do *not* do. He is always true to His Word, and His promises are waiting to be fulfilled in our lives.

> **...and let her own works praise her in the gates.**
> **— Proverbs 31:31**

As I stated previously, if you are looking for honor and appreciation, find it from knowing the Lord. But also, look to the work of your own hands. Your life does not have to shame you. All that you have done, both big and small, can humbly nod with a smile.

My own works have come back to me with tears of joy, saying, "Thank you. Thank you so much."

I guess Jesus meant it when He said, "It is more blessed to give than to receive" (Acts 20:35). It *is* more blessed.

Something so very personal happens deep in the heart of a giver. It is like heaven opens a window and a glimpse of His glory is given. It is strange and wonderful and very divine.

What we do in secret will one day be rewarded openly. So often that happens, but not always. However, if we are truly givers, it really doesn't matter who witnesses our "Good Samaritan" lifestyle. We do all things before Him and for Him.

I hope that on occasion my giving has made the Father happy — even better, that it has caused Him to grin. How cool! Can you imagine making Jesus and the Father grin? I love it. Considering all the Lord has done for me, the least I can do for Him is to be a giver.

And after we've obeyed Him in giving, what does He go ahead and do? He illuminates all things done for Him. Nothing goes unnoticed. And then He starts blessing us all over again and in even greater measure. This God of ours is just *too much*!

Your Own Works Have Something To Say

Your own works will praise you in the public place. Word gets around; people find out. Your own works start applauding you — and all you really know to do at that point is cry.

There is no room for pride. You know you have done nothing, really. Certainly you've done nothing without the Lord's prompting, His provision, His power. It is He who gave you the first seeds to sow anyway.

So you look up to Heaven and smile; then you close your eyes and bow your head in reverence. All you can think about is how the Lord has showered you with kindness all your life, ever since you became a giver. Through it all, it has seemed that *of His goodness there is no end, and His ways are truly past finding out.*

Then suddenly, you remember the age-old question that has resonated through the centuries: "Who can find a virtuous woman?" And from somewhere deep within you, a flash of revelation rises to the surface. You now know that because of God's love for you and by the strength of His grace upon you, the virtuous woman *can* be found — *in you!*

Epilogue:
An Allegory of a Giver

Let me share a separate story now. In another place and another time, a blessing wants to flow.

"Give to her the fruits of her hands" (Prov. 31:31) is a beautiful concept. But I wonder what the day of reward will be like if those hands come wanting but are empty?

That imperative phrase "Give to her" sounds great. We focus in on the word *give*. We know a gift is about to be offered. We breath easy, knowing that at any moment, a "something good" is coming our way. A party is about to begin. Someone's day is ready to be brightened up. But *whose* day? Are all included?

So begins a drama viewed by few but lived by thousands.

❖ ❖ ❖ ❖ ❖ ❖

I hear a stirring in Heaven.

So much commotion is going on.

The Gift-Giver goes to Heaven's mathematicians (a.k.a., Seedtime and Harvest) for an update. "I want to bless her so badly," says the Gift-Giver. "Let Me know right away what is in her account. Then out of her own abundance, you can multiply the sum so I can give back to her." Seedtime and Harvest spend hours calculating, adding, and subtracting. Finally, an average is tallied.

Her day comes. It always comes; it is a clockwork cycle. In Heaven they call it "the Rotation of Rewards" during the round-table discussions. In all these discussions, Gift-Giver, Seedtime, and Harvest are in complete and absolute agreement. The three work very well together; one is never independent of the other two.

She stands there, excited, nervous, anxious with anticipation. She waits to receive, just like all of us stand waiting to receive. She daydreams. How to get all the goodies home and then where to put everything is a nice problem to have.

The huge, palace-like gates open. This is the Realm of Receiving, and at one time or another, everyone enters here. She stands and waits. The gifts are beginning to be passed out. She watches while many receive huge, artistically wrapped gifts. Others carry out small, unimpressive packages.

All those waiting seem relatively happy, although smiles do vary a bit. *My turn is coming,* she sighs. *Here we go.* One nice-sized gift is handed to her from the Gift-Giver. Appreciation and smiles are exchanged. She tenderly takes the beautifully wrapped box and places it gently on the floor, standing up and looking to receive another.

But there are no more gifts for her. She scowls and wonders, *Where did the Gift-Giver go?*

The Gift Giver is gone. He has moved down the line.

Already? she wonders. Baffled and a little agitated, she cannot keep silent. "Excuse me, please! Excuse me! Gift-Giver, is there not more for me?"

She quickly brings her hand to her lips, shocked that she has even spoken. She desperately wishes that she could retrieve the words that had slipped out so impulsively. But it is too late. Silence covers the great hall. All heads now turn in her direction. Embarrassed and shamed, she stumbles over an apology.

The Gift-Giver walks back in her direction. Standing in front of her, He reaches out and wipes away her tears. With the assembly still listening, He says, "Let Me explain — let Me explain to *all* of you." His eyes never leaving hers, He begins.

"I *want* to give; that is who I am. I am the *Gift-Giver.* I want to bless and give abundantly above all you could ask or think. I want to give good portions pressed down, shaken together, and running over. I want your cup to be full to overflowing. There is nothing that brings me more joy than blessing you.

"But, you see," Gift-Giver continued, "I have this agreement with Seedtime and Harvest, and it is this: All blessings and rewards hinge upon a clause that includes eight words — just eight simple words, or four statements, depending on how you look at it."

He clears His throat, realizing that this is not the time to be funny and that no one is laughing.

"That clause states: *"according to; give; with what manner; and if you."*

"That is our law. It is the way of Heaven, and it governs the gifts given on earth. My child," the Gift-Giver says gently as He lifts her fallen chin, "didn't you know that ?"

"No, I didn't know," comes the humbled, hushed response. "I was not familiar with that clause, or with Heaven's law, for that matter. How would I have known?"

Then the Gift-Giver, so gracious and so accommodating, hands her another gift. (How like Him to do that! How precious and predictable!)

"Here," He says to her, "this is just for you. Enjoy it, relish it — but please do read it. Read it as if your peace and all your provisions depend on what you learn. In another time, we will meet again, and we will pick up where we have left off. You will understand more as you study. We will have more to talk about in another season."

The inevitable happened. The seasons changed, and the calendar turned its pages. Life went on, and the days yielded endless opportunities to study the Book the Gift-Giver blessed her with. At first, she thought it would be like boot camp, a grueling challenge. She imagined that the breaking of her stubborn will might prove to be a bloody battle. She was so wrong.

The Book is filled with stories — stories about love and hate, saints and sinners, winning and losing, forgiving and praying. As she reads, she realizes that the entire Book

from start to finish is about *giving.* The Book is about what it really means to be a giver. *How like Him!* she thinks.

As she reads, she also *does.* It becomes fun to bless others. She looks for opportunities to "sow seed," a common phrase and practice found in the Book.

The funny thing was that no matter how much she gave, she could not outgive the Gift-Giver — as if she ever thought she could! But it was fun trying. She laughed often to herself. He heard her and laughed right along with her, sharing the joy she was learning.

In the beginning of this new season, she and Seedtime were not on the same wavelength. They had a major communication problem. She saw him as demanding and thought he lacked understanding as to why she could not always "sow." Seedtime was also a stickler for rules. That particular quality of his irritated her more than once.

Harvest, though, was her favorite from the beginning (besides the Gift-Giver, of course). Harvest is patient and gentle, humble and pure. He wants only to honor Seedtime.

There is no hidden agenda. The greatest joy of Gift-Giver, Seedtime, and Harvest is to bless. Harvest's lifeline is Seedtime, without whom he couldn't even express himself. Seedtime feels the same way about Harvest, and both live for the Gift-Giver.

Harvest taught her how to wait and to love the fruit of one's labor. Both Seedtime and Harvest were relentless — almost overbearing — in their teaching concerning the soil. But she grew to love them both. She changed; she matured; she became like them. *And she waited,* for she now knew all about "due season."

Once again I hear a stirring in heaven; she hears it too.

There is so much commotion going on.

This time when she approaches the gates, she has a smile; she has so much to talk about with the Gift-Giver. She can't wait to see Him. Earlier He had gotten word to her that He had something very special for her and that He would meet her at the gates.

She can see Him from afar. He's standing there, waiting. She runs to Him, and they embrace. They hold hands and walk. She babbles on until she realizes what she is doing.

The Gift-Giver gives her time to share her full-to-over-flowing heart. Then He abruptly stops walking. She hadn't noticed that they had passed through some gates into a garden. She is taken back by the garden's beauty. Stunned, her emotions are awakened by this beautiful place.

There they stand, surrounded by beauty and color. The Gift-Giver starts to laugh. (Or is He crying? I think it is a mixture.) And she is overwhelmed with all kinds of emotion. She looks around, biting her lower lip, wiping away tears, hugging Him, laughing, then crying some more. The next few moments seem to take on a life of their own. Again and again she composes herself, only to start up all over again. Finally, she just sits down and weeps. The Gift-Giver sits with her and weeps with her.

She knows what surrounds her, and, of course, He knows that she knows. She knows the jubilation she hears is the sound of her own works praising her. Her own giving now greets her; her own love now lauds her; her own kindness kisses her so sweetly.

She lowers her eyes, embarrassed. The Gift-Giver lifts her fallen chin and says, "Well done, My good and faithful servant.

"This is all yours," He continues, waving His hand to include all the beauty surrounding them. "You have entered into My joy. You have become a giver — a gift-giver."

...Let her own works praise her in the gates.
— Proverbs 31:31

Endnotes

Chapter One

[1] *Merriam Webster Dictionary* (Philippines: G. and C. Merriam Co.,1974), p. 559.

[2] *The New Open Bible* (Nashville: Thomas Nelson Publishers, 1990) p. 711.

[3] Ibid., p. 711, 717.

[4] Ibid.

[5] Ibid.

[6] *Wilmington's Book of Bible Lists* (Wheaton, Illinois: Tyndale House Publishers, Inc., 1987), p. 34.

[7] *The New Open Bible*, p. 703.

[8] *American Heritage College Dictionary* (Boston: Houghton-Mifflin Company, 1993), p. 48.

Chapter Three

[9] Packer, Tenney, and White, ed., GUIDEPOSTS, *The Bible Almanac* (Carmel, New York: Thomas Nelson Publishers, 1990), p. 477.

[10] Ibid., pp. 477-479.

Chapter Six

[11] *American Heritage College Dictionary*, p. 1102.

[12] Ibid.

Chapter Twelve

[13] *The Bible Almanac*, p. 476.

Chapter Fifteen

[14] *American Heritage College Dictionary*, p. 1523.

[15] James Strong, "Greek Dictionary of the New Testament," *Strong's Exhaustive Concordance of the Bible* (Madison, New Jersey: World Bible Publishers, Inc., 1986), p. 71, #3789.

Chapter Seventeen

[16] *American Heritage College Dictionary*, p. 148.

[17] James Strong, "Hebrew Dictionary of the Old Testament," *Strong's Exhaustive Concordance of the Bible* (Madison, New Jersey: World Bible Publishers, Inc., 1986), p. 21, #833.

Chapter Eighteen

[18] "Greek Dictionary of the New Testament," *Strong's Exhaustive Concordance of the Bible*, p. 5, #25.

Chapter Nineteen

[19] *Hebrew-Greek Key Study Bible* (Chattanooga: AMG Publishers, 1984), p. 41, #2580.

[20] *American Heritage College Dictionary*, p. 236.

For Further Information

For further information
about Keys to Freedom Ministries
or for additional copies of this book,
please call or write:

Shoddy Chase
Keys to Freedom Ministries
P. O. Box 91995
Lakeland, FL 33804-1995
(941) 683-3984